TIME PASSAGES

By Robert Burtt & Bill Main

"The key to unlocking the door to our future opens with a journey into the past."

Robert Burtt & Bill Main

THIRD PRINTING

Rock Hudson and Dorothy Malone star in the new film "Written On The Wind".

Sunday	Monday	Tuesday	Wednesday	Thursday	Friday	Saturday
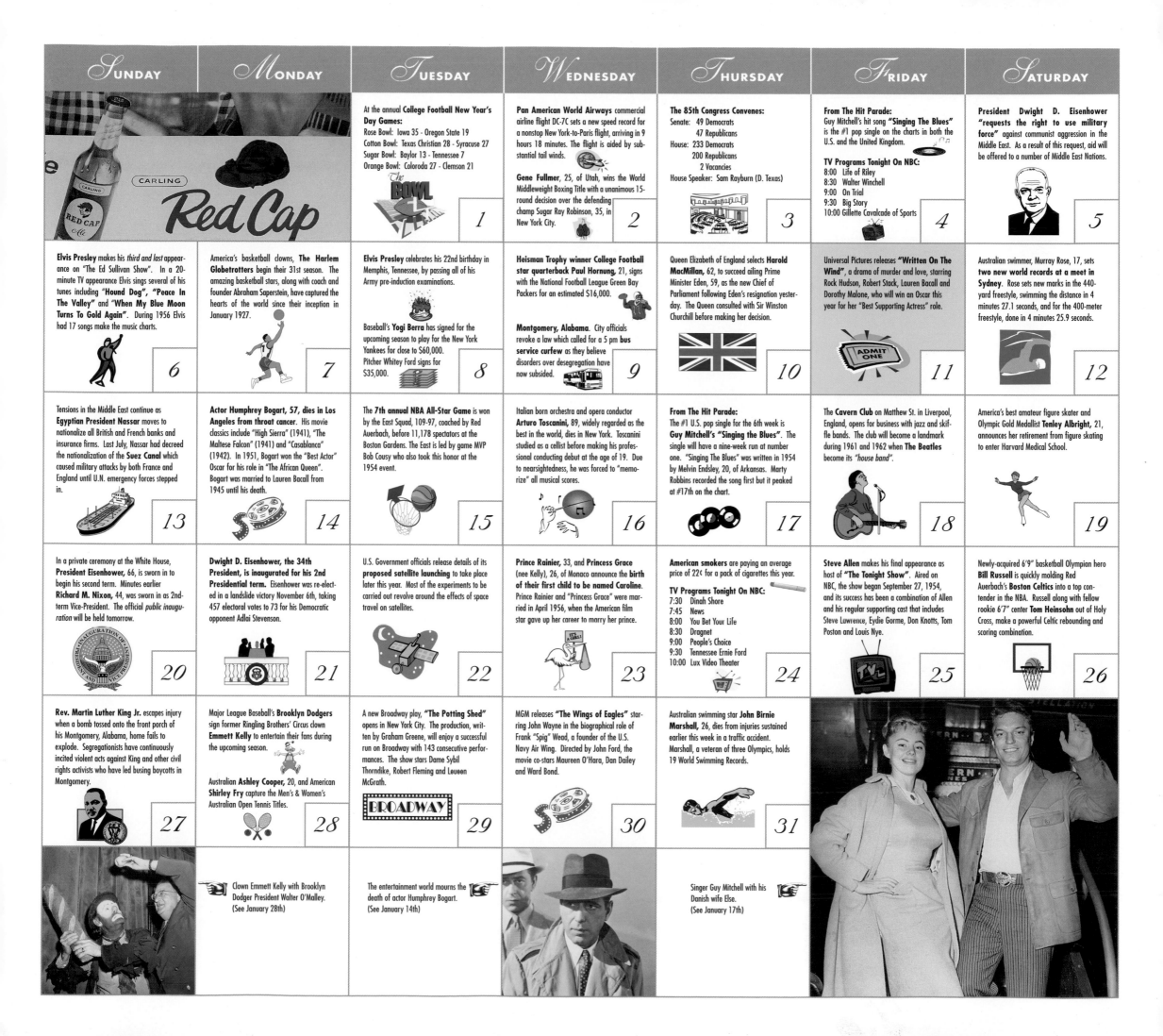 CARLING Red Cap		At the annual **College Football New Year's Day Games:** Rose Bowl: Iowa 35 - Oregon State 19 Cotton Bowl: Texas Christian 28 - Syracuse 27 Sugar Bowl: Baylor 13 - Tennessee 7 Orange Bowl: Coloroda 27 - Clemson 21 **1**	**Pan American World Airways** commercial airline flight DC-7C sets a new speed record for a nonstop New York-to-Paris flight, arriving in 9 hours 18 minutes. The flight is aided by substantial tail winds. **Gene Fullmer,** 25, of Utah, wins the World Middleweight Boxing Title with a unanimous 15-round decision over the defending champ Sugar Ray Robinson, 35, in New York City. **2**	**The 85th Congress Convenes:** Senate: 49 Democrats 47 Republicans House: 233 Democrats 200 Republicans 2 Vacancies House Speaker: Sam Rayburn (D. Texas) **3**	**From The Hit Parade:** Guy Mitchell's hit song **"Singing The Blues"** is the #1 pop single on the charts in both the U.S. and the United Kingdom. **TV Programs Tonight On NBC:** 8:00 Life of Riley 8:30 Walter Winchell 9:00 On Trial 9:30 Big Story 10:00 Gillette Cavalcade of Sports **4**	**President Dwight D. Eisenhower** "requests the right to use military force" against communist aggression in the Middle East. As a result of this request, aid will be offered to a number of Middle East Nations. **5**
Elvis Presley makes his *third and last* appearance on "The Ed Sullivan Show". In a 20-minute TV appearance Elvis sings several of his tunes including **"Hound Dog", "Peace In The Valley"** and **"When My Blue Moon Turns To Gold Again"**. During 1956 Elvis had 17 songs make the music charts. **6**	America's basketball clowns, **The Harlem Globetrotters** begin their 31st season. The amazing basketball stars, along with coach and founder Abraham Saperstein, have captured the hearts of the world since their inception in January 1927. **7**	**Elvis Presley** celebrates his 22nd birthday in Memphis, Tennessee, by passing all of his Army pre-induction examinations. Baseball's **Yogi Berra** has signed for the upcoming season to play for the New York Yankees for close to $60,000. Pitcher Whitey Ford signs for $35,000. **8**	Heisman Trophy winner College Football star quarterback Paul Hornung, 21, signs with the National Football League Green Bay Packers for an estimated $16,000. **Montgomery, Alabama.** City officials revoke a law which called for a 5 pm **bus service curfew** as they believe disorders over desegregation have now subsided. **9**	Queen Elizabeth of England selects **Harold MacMillan,** 62, to succeed ailing Prime Minister Eden, 59, as the new Chief of Parliament following Eden's resignation yesterday. The Queen consulted with Sir Winston Churchill before making her decision. **10**	Universal Pictures releases **"Written On The Wind"**, a drama of murder and love, starring Rock Hudson, Robert Stack, Lauren Bacall and Dorothy Malone, who will win an Oscar this year for her "Best Supporting Actress" role. **11**	Australian swimmer, Murray Rose, 17, sets **two new world records at a meet in Sydney.** Rose sets new marks in the 440-yard freestyle, swimming the distance in 4 minutes 27.1 seconds, and for the 400-meter freestyle, done in 4 minutes 25.9 seconds. **12**
Tensions in the Middle East continue as **Egyptian President Nassar** moves to nationalize all British and French banks and insurance firms. Last July, Nassar had decreed the nationalization of the **Suez Canal** which caused military attacks by both France and England until U.N. emergency forces stepped in. **13**	Actor **Humphrey Bogart,** 57, dies in Los Angeles from throat cancer. His movie classics include "High Sierra" (1941), "The Maltese Falcon" (1941) and "Casablanca" (1942). In 1951, Bogart won the "Best Actor" Oscar for his role in "The African Queen". Bogart was married to Lauren Bacall from 1945 until his death. **14**	The 7th annual NBA All-Star Game is won by the East Squad, 109-97, coached by Red Auerbach, before 11,178 spectators at the Boston Gardens. The East is led by game MVP Bob Cousy who also took this honor at the 1954 event. **15**	Italian born orchestra and opera conductor **Arturo Toscanini,** 89, widely regarded as the best in the world, dies in New York. Toscanini studied as a cellist before making his profesional conducting debut at the age of 19. Due to nearsightedness, he was forced to "memorize" all musical scores. **16**	**From The Hit Parade:** The #1 U.S. pop single for the 6th week is **Guy Mitchell's "Singing the Blues".** The single will have a nine-week run at number one. "Singing The Blues" was written in 1954 by Melvin Endsley, 20, of Arkansas. Marty Robbins recorded the song first but it peaked at #17 on the chart. **17**	The **Cavern Club** on Matthew St. in Liverpool, England, opens for business with jazz and skifle bands. The club will become a landmark during 1961 and 1962 when **The Beatles** become its *"house band"*. **18**	America's best amateur figure skater and Olympic Gold Medallist **Tenley Albright,** 21, announces her retirement from figure skating to enter Harvard Medical School. **19**
In a private ceremony at the White House, **President Eisenhower,** 66, is sworn in to begin his second term. Minutes earlier **Richard M. Nixon,** 44, was sworn in as 2nd-term Vice-President. The official *public inauguration* will be held tomorrow. **20**	**Dwight D. Eisenhower, the 34th President,** is inaugurated for his 2nd Presidential term. Eisenhower was re-elected in a landslide victory November 6th, taking 457 electoral votes to 73 for his Democratic opponent Adlai Stevenson. **21**	U.S. Government officials release details of its **proposed satellite launching** to take place later this year. Most of the experiments to be carried out revolve around the effects of space travel on satellites. **22**	**Prince Rainier,** 33, and **Princess Grace** (nee Kelly), 26, of Monaco announce the **birth** of their first child to be named **Caroline.** Prince Rainier and "Princess Grace" were married in April 1956, when the American film star gave up her career to marry her prince. **23**	**American smokers** are paying an average price of 22¢ for a pack of cigarettes this year. **TV Programs Tonight On NBC:** 7:30 Dinah Shore 7:45 News 8:00 You Bet Your Life 8:30 Dragnet 9:00 People's Choice 9:30 Tennessee Ernie Ford 10:00 Lux Video Theater **24**	**Steve Allen** makes his final appearance as host of **"The Tonight Show"**. Aired on NBC, the show began September 27, 1954, and its success has been a combination of Allen and his regular supporting cast that includes Steve Lawrence, Eydie Gorme, Don Knotts, Tom Poston and Louis Nye. **25**	Newly-acquired 6'9" basketball Olympian hero **Bill Russell** is quickly molding Red Auerbach's **Boston Celtics** into a top contender in the NBA. Russell along with fellow rookie 6'7" center **Tom Heinsohn** out of Holy Cross, make a powerful Celtic rebounding and scoring combination. **26**
Rev. Martin Luther King Jr. escapes injury when a bomb tossed onto the front porch of his Montgomery, Alabama, home fails to explode. Segregationists have continuously incited violent acts against King and other civil rights activists who have led busing boycotts in Montgomery. **27**	Major League Baseball's **Brooklyn Dodgers** sign former Ringling Brothers' Circus clown **Emmett Kelly** to entertain their fans during the upcoming season. Australian **Ashley Cooper,** 20, and American **Shirley Fry** capture the Men's & Women's Australian Open Tennis Titles. **28**	A new Broadway play, **"The Potting Shed"** opens in New York City. The production, written by Graham Greene, will enjoy a successful run on Broadway with 143 consecutive performances. The show stars Dame Sybil Thorndike, Robert Fleming and Leueen McGrath. **BROADWAY** **29**	MGM releases **"The Wings of Eagles"** starring John Wayne in the biographical role of Frank "Spig" Wead, a founder of the U.S. Navy Air Wing. Directed by John Ford, the movie co-stars Maureen O'Hara, Dan Dailey and Ward Bond. **30**	Australian swimming star **John Birnie Marshall,** 26, dies from injuries sustained earlier this week in a traffic accident. Marshall, a veteran of three Olympics, holds 19 World Swimming Records. **31**		
	Clown Emmett Kelly with Brooklyn Dodger President Walter O'Malley. (See January 28th)	The entertainment world mourns the death of actor Humphrey Bogart. (See January 14th)		Singer Guy Mitchell with his Danish wife Else. (See January 17th)		

Actress Elizabeth Taylor marries movie producer Mike Todd.

Sunday	Monday	Tuesday	Wednesday	Thursday	Friday	Saturday
		Leonard Ross,11, shows off his cheque for $64,000 which he won on the television show "The $64,000 Challenge". (See February 11th) Philco "Slender Seventeener" Table Set... sells for $159.95.			MGM Motion Pictures releases a new film, **"The Iron Petticoat"**, starring Katharine Hepburn as a Soviet whose communist ideals fade while in the West. The film co-stars Bob Hope, Noelle Middleton and James Robertson. **1**	Actress **Elizabeth Taylor**, 24, marries movie producer **Mike Todd**, 54, in a ceremony near Acapulco, Mexico. It is the 3rd marriage for both Taylor and Todd. Taylor was first married in 1950 to Conrad Hilton Jr. and then in 1952 to Michael Wilding. **2**
Israel responds to the **United Nations General Assembly** demands that Israel withdraw from Egyptian Territory. Israel claims that no withdrawals have been made since Egypt has not guaranteed to stop its belligerence and sea blockade of Israel. **3**	Bishop, Virginia: A **tragic mining disaster** occurs as an underground explosion at a Pocahontas Fuel Company mine kills 37 men. It is the worst U.S. mining disaster since an Illinois accident in 1951 claimed 119 lives. The #1 song on the Country and Western music chart is **"Young Love"** by Sonny James. **4**	The **Civil Aeronautics Board** bans all test flights over congested areas following a recent midair collision that fell onto a Pacoima, California, Jr. High School yard, killing 2 while injuring 70 others. New York center fielder **Mickey Mantle**, 25, signs a new contract to play for the defending World Champion Yankees. The popular star signs for close to $60,000. **5**	**Jewish survivors** of the **Auschwitz Concentration Camp** who were slave laborers in I.G. Farben factories, will each receive a settlement of upto $1,190 as worked out by West Germany and the Jewish Material Claims Group. **6**	A new Broadway play, **"Visit To A Small Planet"** opens in New York City. The comedy, written by Gore Vidal, will enjoy a successful run on Broadway with 388 performances. The play stars Eddie Mayehoff, Sarah Marshall and Philip Coolidge. BROADWAY **7**	Retiring Assistant Defense Secretary for Research and Development, Dr. Clifford Furnes estimates that an **unmanned rocket will travel to the Moon within 10 years**, while a manned vehicle will be possible within 25 years. **8**	**From The Hit Parade:** The Top 5 Pop Singles are: 1) "Too Much" - Elvis Presley 2) "Young Love" - Sonny James 3) "Don't Forbid Me" - Pat Boone 4) "Young Love" - Tab Hunter 5) "Singing The Blues" - Guy Mitchell **9**
American author **Laura Ingalls Wilder** dies at age 90. At the age of 65, Wilder began writing the "Little House" novels. Her most famous, **"Little House On The Prairie"**, was published in 1935 and it will become the basis of a hit TV series that will premiere on September 11th, 1974. **10**	Leonard Ross, 11, from California wins the grand prize on the popular CBS television show **"The $64,000 Challenge"**, answering a final question on the stock market. In April 1956 Leonard won $100,000 on NBC's "The Big Surprise". **11**	Federal District Judge Walter Hoffman hands down an order in Norfolk and Newport News, Virginia, ordering the two cities to begin **desegregating their public schools** by mid-August. Similar rulings in Kentucky and Tennessee are also ordered. **12**	**Tennessee Attorney General George McCanless** charges that the new civil rights legislation now before the House is unnecessary and will only lead to "further invasion of areas of government that properly belong to the States". The Georgia Senate unanimously passes a bill to **ban all interracial sports** practices or competitions within the State. **13**	Prison officials at **San Quentin** place convict and author **Caryl Chessman** in solitary confinement. Officials, while searching his cell, found a manuscript for his 3rd book "The Face Of Justice". His writing for publication had been banned by state authorities. **14**	American consumers are paying an average price of 55¢ for a **5-lb bag of sugar**. **TV Programs Tonight On CBS:** 7:30 My Friend Flicka 8:00 West Point 8:30 Zane Grey Theater 9:00 The Crusader 9:30 Schlitz Playhouse 10:00 The Lineup 10:30 Person To Person **15**	Despite pressure from the United States, **Israel continues to refuse to withdraw from Egypt** until it receives guarantees from Egypt that ships can travel without incident through the Gulf of Aqaba. **16**
Everett "Cotton" Owens of Spartanburg, S.C., wins the NASCAR Grand National Rally at Daytona Beach for hardtop sports cars, driving his 1957 Pontiac to victory. Milwaukee Braves pitcher **Warren Spahn**, 36, signs a new one-year contract for the upcoming season, estimated to be worth $50,000. **17**	The **State of Georgia** House votes 107-33 in favor of a resolution to be sent to the Senate calling for the immediate **impeachment of six U.S. Supreme Court Justices** who had unanimously voted in the recent school desegregation rulings. **18**	American playwright **Arthur Miller** has been indicted by a Federal Grand Jury in Washington D.C. The husband of actress Marilyn Monroe refuses to inform the House Un-American Activities Committee of people he had seen a at a Communist meeting he attended during 1947. **19**	**From The Hit Parade:** The #1 United Kingdom pop single is Tab Hunter's **"Young Love"**. The hit will stay on top of the U.K. charts until April 10th when Lonnie Donegan's "Cumberland Gap" will take over. **TV Programs Tonight On ABC:** 7:30 Disneyland 8:30 Navy Log 9:00 Ozzie and Harriet **20**	Warner Brothers releases a new film, **"The Spirit of St. Louis"**, starring Jimmy Stewart as aviation hero Charles Lindbergh who made the first solo trans-Atlantic flight during 1927. The film is directed by Billy Wilder. ADMIT ONE **21**	Actor **Robert Young** celebrates his 50th birthday. Final details are being completed to allow the **Minneapolis Lakers** of the NBA to be sold for $150,000. The new owners, Marty Marion and Milton Fischmann, plan to move the franchise if a local purchaser is not found within the next 30 days. **22**	The U.S. Supreme Court rules 6-3 that the **National Football League** is within the coverage of antitrust laws. Former Detroit guard Bill Radvich had sued the NFL for $35,000 because the league had refused to let him switch from Detroit to L.A. FBI officials announce that **65 executions** took place in 1956 compared to 76 in 1955. 52 of the deaths were for murder. **23**
After a **seven-month strike** by Ohio **Telephone** workers, a settlement is reached, but not before more than 500 cables had been cut during the bitter and violent strike. **TV Programs Tonight On NBC:** 7:00 777th Bengal Lancers 7:30 Circus Boy 8:00 The Steve Allen Show 9:00 The Alcoa Hour 10:00 Loretta Young **24**	George "Bugs" Moran, 64, the former gangster opponent of Al Capone during the late 1920's, dies of lung cancer while serving a robbery jail term in Fort Leavenworth, Kansas. **Buddy Holly and The Crickets** record "That'll Be The Day" in New Mexico. **25**	A California State Investigation Committee is attempting to determine whether or not singer **Frank Sinatra** was involved in the 1954 raid on Marilyn Monroe's apartment to gather evidence of adultery for her ex-husband Joe DiMaggio. **26**	A **130-carat cut diamond** valued at $2 million goes on display at Harry Winston of New York . The diamond was cut from a 426-carat "raw diamond" discovered in South Africa 3 years ago. **TV Programs Tonight On CBS:** 7:30 Giant Step 8:00 The Arthur Godfrey Show 9:00 The Millionaire 9:30 I've Got A Secret **27**	Jockey **Johnny Longden**, 47, rides his 5,000th winner at Santa Anita in California. Longden began his illustrious career 30 years ago in 1927. The Women's World Figure Skating Championships in Colorado Springs conclude as Carol Heiss, 17, of the U.S. places 1st. **28**		

36-year-old Milwaukee Braves pitching ace Warren Spahn signs a new contract for the upcoming season. (See February 17th)

1957 Lincoln Premiere 4-Door with landau hardtop.

Jockey Johnny Longden, aboard "Bente" on the rail, wins his 5,000th career race. (See February 28th)

Ingrid Bergman wins the "Best Actress" Oscar for her performance in the film "Anastasia".

Sunday	Monday	Tuesday	Wednesday	Thursday	Friday	Saturday
Post Toasties Corn Flakes	Many Americans start their day with Post "Toasties Corn Flakes". "You'll Never Get Rich" star **Phil Silvers** wins the "Best Series" Television Emmy. (See March 16th)		Musician Muddy Waters releases his record "I Got My Mojo Working". (See March 1st)		Chicago, Illinois: Musician "Muddy Waters" releases his single **"I Got My Mojo Working"** backed with "Rock Me" on the Chess Record label. Entertainer **Dinah Shore** celebrates her 40th birthday. **1**	The Men's World Figure Skating Championships in Colorado Springs conclude as David Jenkins, 20, of the U.S. finishes first with teammate Tim Brown placing second and Canada's Charles Snelling finishing third. **2**
Vice-President Richard Nixon arrives in Accra to represent the U.S. at the birth of Ghana as an independent nation. Golfer Jimmy Demaret, 45, wins the $2,000 first prize in the **Baton Rouge Louisiana Open**. **3**	Israeli forces are withdrawing from the **Gaza Strip** and other areas of Sinai following an agreement announced earlier by Israeli Foreign Minister Golda Meir to the U.N. General Assembly. Israel's Army Chief General Moshe Dayan turns over the area to the U.N. Emergency Forces. **4**	**Sweden** captures the World Ice Hockey Championship in Moscow. The victory is tarnished however as Canada, the U.S. and several European countries refused to participate in protest against "Soviet repression" in the Hungarian Revolution. **5**	**Fats Domino** continues to dominate the R&B charts with the #1 R&B song "Blueberry Hill" followed by "Blue Monday". Musician **Bill Haley** celebrates his 30th birthday. **6**	Motorcar enthusiasts are paying an average of 31¢ per **gallon of gasoline** this year. The #1 song on the Country and Western music chart is **"There You Go"** by Johnny Cash. In 1956, Cash had a #1 song also with "I Walk The Line". **7**	The #1 TV show in the U.S. for the fourth year is CBS's **"I Love Lucy"** starring Lucille Ball, Desi Arnaz, Vivian Vance and William Frawley. The popular sitcom first debuted in October 1951. **8**	Actor **Henry Fonda**, 51, marries Italian Contessa Afdera Franchetti, 24, in New York. It is the fourth marriage for Fonda. **TV Programs Tonight On NBC:** 7:30 People Are Funny 8:00 The Perry Como Show 9:00 Caesar's Hour 10:00 George Gobel 10:30 Your Hit Parade **9**
Robert Strom, 10, of New York wins the top prize on CBS's hit TV show "**The $64,000 Question**" with his correct answer on "science". The popular program is about to announce a new limit of $256,000 if contestants wish to risk doubling their winnings up to the new limit. **10**	Columbia University English instructor **Charles Van Doren**, 31, wins $129,000 as he ends his 14-week appearance on the NBC-TV quiz show "Twenty One". The first man to fly over both the North and South Poles during 1928 and 1929, explorer and aviator **Rear Adm. Richard E. Byrd**, 68, dies in Boston. **11**	Industrialist film producer **Howard Hughes**, 51, marries actress Jean Peters, 30, in Las Vegas. For both Hughes and Peters it is their 2nd time to the altar. **TV Programs Tonight On CBS:** 7:30 Name That Tune 8:00 You'll Never Get Rich 8:30 The Brothers 9:00 Herb Shriner 9:30 Red Skelton **12**	Kansas City: At the NCAA Championship, **North Carolina defeats Kansas 54-53** in the third period of overtime. N.C.'s Lennie Rosenbluth is high scorer with 140 points in five games while Kansas sophomore Wilt Chamberlain is named MVP. **13**	Newspapers in the U.S. report that **Teamsters Union** VP Jimmy Hoffa, 44, has been arrested on charges of federal bribery. Hoffa is accused of hiring attorney John Chesty for purposes of supplying Hoffa with confidential reports about the government's committee's inquiry into alleged Teamster racketeering. **14**	Convicted kidnapper and murderer **Burton Abbott** is executed in San Quentin's gas chamber for his 1955 crime against Stephanie Bryan, 14, of Berkley, California. Two minutes after his execution, Governor Goodwin Knight calls the prison to secure a temporary reprieve. **15**	The annual television **Emmy Awards** are presented including: Best Single Program: "Requiem For A HeavyWeight" Best Series: "You'll Never Get Rich" (Phil Silvers) Best Female Personality: Dinah Shore Best Actor: Robert Young ("Father Knows Best") **16**
TV Programs Tonight On CBS: 7:00 Lassie 7:30 Jack Benny 8:00 The Ed Sullivan Show 9:00 G.E. Theater 9:30 Alfred Hitchcock 10:00 The $64,000 Challenge 10:30 What's My Line? **17**	NBC-TV premieres a new 30-minute western adventure series "**The Tales of Wells Fargo**" starring Dale Robertson as Jim Hardie, a trouble-shooter in the 1860's who handles investigations for the Wells Fargo Gold Transporters. **18**	Rock and roll stars **Bill Haley and The Comets** return from an 11-week tour of Australia, Europe and the United Kingdom where they performed before over 500,000 fans. Rock and roll shows have become the rage around the world and its best performers are using tours to promote record sales. **19**	Paramount Pictures premieres a new film, **"Fear Strikes Out"**, starring Anthony Perkins as Boston Red Sox star "Jimmy Piersall" who was pushed to a breakdown by the pressures to excel in America's favorite sport. His overzealous father is played by Karl Malden. **20**	A British Parliamentary Act signed by Queen Elizabeth II **establishes life imprisonment as the most severe penalty for murder**. The debate on whether or not to abolish capital punishment will become a most important issue in countries all around the world. **21**	The city of **San Francisco** suffers its worst earthquake since the 1906 disaster as six tremors over a four-hour period rock the California city. Fortunately, no deaths are reported this day. **22**	**President Eisenhower and Prime Minister Harold MacMillan** of Great Britain continue their meetings in Bermuda as the two world leaders discuss opportunities to mend the English-U.S. relations damaged recently by policy differences in the Middle East. **23**
A **severe blizzard** strikes the midwestern and southwestern States with reported snowdrifts up to 30 feet high. Six passenger trains and thousands of travellers are stranded. At least 40 deaths have been directly attributed to the blizzard which is now in its third day. **24**	A report on the **effects of cigarette smoking** is leaked to the media. The report says that "the sum total of scientific evidence establishes beyond reasonable doubt that cigarette smoking is a major factor in the rapidly increasing incidence of lung cancer". **DANGER CAUSES CANCER** **25**	**NBA Season Leaders:** Scoring: Paul Arizin (Phil) 1817 pts Rebounding: Maurice Stokes (Roch) 1256 (a new record) Assists: 5th time Bob Cousy (Boston) 478 **26**	**The 29th Academy Award Oscars** are presented including: Best Picture: "Around The World in 80 Days" Best Director: George Stevens for "Giant" Best Actress: Ingrid Bergman for "Anastasia" Best Actor: Yul Brynner for "The King and I" **HOLLYWOOD MOVIES** **27**	**NHL Season Leaders:** Points: Gordie Howe (Detroit) 89 (5th time) Goals: Gordie Howe (Detroit) 44 (4th time) Assists: Ted Lindsay (Detroit) 55 (3rd time) Goals-Against Avg: Jacques Plante (Mtl) 2.02 Penalty Minutes: Gus Mortson (Chicago) 147 (4th time) **28**	The first **U.S. National Curling Championships** are held in the Chicago Stadium in Illinois. Ten teams compete for the crown which is captured by the Hibbling Curling Club from Minnesota, skipped by Harold Lauber. **29**	The visiting St. Louis Hawks led by star scorer Bob Pettit stun the heavily-favored Boston Celtics 125-123 in double overtime to take the early series lead in the **National Basketball Association (NBA)** Best-of-Seven Championship Finals. **30**
The home-court **Boston Celtics** rebound to defeat the St. Louis Hawks 119-99 to even their series at one game apiece. Celtic's Bob Cousy, Bill Russel and Tom Heinsohn dominate tonight's game. **31**		Quiz Show winner Charles Van Doren with his future wife Geraldine Ann Berstein whom he will marry on April 17th. (See April 11th)	**CREME FORMULA MISS CLAIROL** The Johnson 35-hp Golden Javelin sells for $625. More women use "Miss Clairol" than any other hair colorant.	The Johnson 35-hp Golden Javelin sells for $625. More women use "Miss Clairol" than any other hair colorant.		

Henry Fonda with an all-star cast in the new film "Twelve Angry Men".

Sunday	Monday	Tuesday	Wednesday	Thursday	Friday	Saturday
	Cadence Records releases a new record **"Bye, Bye Love"** by The Everly Brothers. The song will eventually hit #1 on the Country and Western chart and #2 on the pop record chart. **TV Programs Tonight On ABC:** 7:30 Bold Journey 8:00 Make Room For Daddy 8:30 Voice Of Firestone 9:00 Bishop Sheen **1**	**Texas**: A violent tornado rips through the Dallas area killing at least 9 people and injuring close to 500 others. **TV Programs Tonight On ABC:** 7:30 Cheyenne 8:30 Wyatt Earp 9:00 Broken Arrow 9:30 Cavalcade Theater 10:00 It's Polka Time **2**	Dancer **Gene Kelly**, 44, is divorced by actress Betsy Blair, 33, in Las Vegas, Nevada. According to A.C. Nielsen the **Top 5** watched TV Shows Are: 1) I Love Lucy 2) The Ed Sullivan Show 3) General Electric Theater 4) The $64,000 Question 5) December Bride **3**	**Rising postal costs** threaten to curtail services provided by the Post Office, including Saturday mail deliveries. Postmaster General Arthur Summerfield approaches the government for $47 million in additional funds. **4**	Government officials announce that **Israel intends to challenge Egypt's Suez Canal blockade** by attempting to send an Israeli-flag-bearing vessel through the canal. Vice-President **Richard Nixon** reports to President Eisenhower on his recent 3-week official visit to 9 African states. He urges for American action to maintain the independence of African countries. **5**	The **Montreal Canadiens** clip the visiting **Boston Bruins 5-1** to take a 1-0 lead in their NHL finals. Maurice Richard scores a record 3 second-period goals and four overall to lead Montreal. **St. Louis Hawks edge the Boston Celtics** 100-98 to take a 2-1 lead in their NBA finals. **6**
Augusta, Georgia: Doug Ford, 34, wins the **21st Masters Golf Tournament**. His 72-hole total of 282 gives Ford the $8,750 first prize, edging out 3-time champion Sam Snead. **Boston Celtics edge the St. Louis Hawks** 123-118 to tie their NBA series at two games apiece. **7**	According to a recent Gallup poll, **fewer Americans are now using alcoholic beverages**. The recent study indicates that 58% of Americans now drink, down from 67% during 1945. The #1 song on the Country and Western music chart is **"Gone"** by **Ferlin Husky**. **8**	Anchored by goaltender Jacques Plante's shutout, **the Canadiens edge the visiting Bruins 1-0** on a goal by Jean Beliveau to take a two-game lead in their NHL finals. **The Boston Celtics thump the St. Louis Hawks 124-109** to take a 3-2 series lead in their NBA finals. **9**	The daughter of actor and former Olympic swimmer Buster Crabbe, **Caren Lynn Crabbe**, 20, dies in Hollywood of malnutrition caused by a "nervous disorder" associated with obsession about not becoming overweight. **From the Hit Parade:** The #1 pop song in the U.S. is "Round and Round" by Perry Como. **10**	The visiting Canadiens, led by **"Boom Boom" Geoffrion** with two first-period goals, defeat the Bruins 4-2 to take a commanding 3-0 series lead in their NHL Stanley Cup finals series. The home-court **St. Louis Hawks** edge the **Boston Celtics** 96-94 to even the NBA Basketball finals at three games apiece. **11**	**Tragedy strikes Japan** when an overloaded wooden ferry capsizes killing 96 off the coast of Onomichi. In another mishap, an additional 18 people die when an **avalanche** destroys a number of coal mining huts near Niigata. **12**	A large American television audience witnesses perhaps the greatest basketball game of all time as the home-court **Boston Celtics nip the visiting St. Louis Hawks** 125-123 in double overtime to win the dramatic seventh and deciding game of their NBA Basketball Championships. **13**
Facing elimination, the Bruins, coached by **Milt Schmidt**, defeat the visiting Canadiens 2-0, backstopped by goalie Don Simmons who gets the shutout. "Mac" MacKell scores both the goals for the Bruins. **14**	United Artists releases a new film **"Twelve Angry Men"** with screenplay by Reginald Rose, starring Henry Fonda, Lee J. Cobb, E.G. Marshall, Martin Balsam, Jack Warden, Ed Begley, George Voskovec, Robert Webber, Jack Klugman, Edward Binns, John Fielder and Joseph Sweeny. Sidney Lumet makes his feature film debut as a director. **15**	The **Montreal Canadiens**, coached by Toe Blake, win their 2nd consecutive **Stanley Cup** with a 5-1 win over the visiting Boston Bruins. Bernie Geoffrion leads all scorers in the play-offs with 11 goals and 18 points. Jacques Plante leads all goalies with a 1.80-goals-against average over 10 games. **16**	**From The Hit Parade:** The Top 5 Pop Singles are: 1) "All Shook Up" - Elvis Presley 2) "Little Darlin'" - Diamonds 3) "Party Doll" - Buddy Knox 4) "Round and Round" - Perry Como 5) "Butterfly" - Andy Williams **17**	The **Florida Senate** completes legislative action on a resolution declaring Supreme Court school desegregation decisions null and void. **President Eisenhower** flies to Augusta, Georgia, for 10 days of golf and relaxation at the Augusta National Golf Club. The President's love of golf has greatly added to golf's popularity with Americans. **18**	The oldest footrace in the U.S., the **Boston Marathon** is held for the 60th time with **John J. Kelley**, 26, of Connecticut winning in a record-breaking time of 2 hours 20 minutes 5 seconds. Finally, after a string of twelve foreign wins, Kelley brings the title back to the U.S. **19**	Soviet Premier Bulganin writes to British Prime Minister MacMillan calling for a **halt to all hydrogen bomb tests**. The **Mayflower II**, a replica of the 1620 Pilgrim vessel, leaves Plymouth, England, for Plymouth, Massachusetts. **20**
Winners of the **11th annual Tony Awards** include: Best Actress: Margaret Leighton for "Separate Tables" Best Actor: Fredric March for "Long Day's Journey Into Night" Best Play: "Long Day's Journey Into Night" by Eugene O'Neill Best Musical: "My Fair Lady" **BROADWAY** **21**	The **First NBA All-Star Team** named for the 1956-57 season is: Paul Arizin - Philadelphia Dolph Schayes - Syracuse Bob Pettit - St. Louis Bob Cousy - Boston Bill Sharman - Boston **22**	According to a Polish newspaper, during the last five years the **Soviet Union has now lost 40 mountain climbers** attempting to scale Mt. Everest, the highest peak in the world. New Zealand's Sir Edmond Hillary became the 1st man to scale the peak in May 1953. **23**	The first United States vessel since October 1956, passes through the **Suez Canal**, paying an Egyptian "toll fee" of $10,295 under protest. TV Actress **Nanette Fabray** marries movie writer Ronald MacDougall in N.Y. **24**	Television star **Ricky Nelson**, 16, releases his first record "Teenager's Romance" that will sell 60,000 copies in the first three days! Nelson's popularity is largely due to his appearances on the weekly TV series "The Adventures Of Ozzie and Harriet" that premiered in October 1952. **25**	The **NBA Rookie Of The Year** for 1956-57 season is Boston Celtic **Tom Heinsohn** whose Celtics finished first with a 48-28 record. Heinsohn was picked up by the Celtics as their #1 pick during the 1956 draft out of Holy Cross University. **26**	Palo Alto, California, pole vaulter **Bob Gutowski** of Occidental College establishes a **new pole vault world record**, leaping 15' 8 1/4", breaking the former mark of 15' 7 3/4" set by Cornelius Warmerdam. **27**
Americans who **invest their savings** in local banks this year will receive an average of 3.2% interest on a regular savings account. American golfer **Billy Casper Jr.**, captures 1st place in the $30,000 Kentucky Derby Open in Louisville. Casper receives $4,300 for the victory. Earlier this year Casper received $2,000 for winning the Phoenix Open. **28**	The United States Interior Department awards a $108-million contract for construction of the **Glen Canyon Dam**, the first major part of the Upper Colorado River Project. **29**	The NBA Podoloff Cup awarded to the league's **Most Valuable Player**, as voted by the players themselves, goes to Boston Celtics **Bob Cousy**. Cousy first played for the Celtics in 1950-51 and this season led the league in assists with 478 for a 7.4 average. **30**		Boston Celtic's Bob Cousy receives his NBA All-Star Game MVP trophy. (See April 30th)		

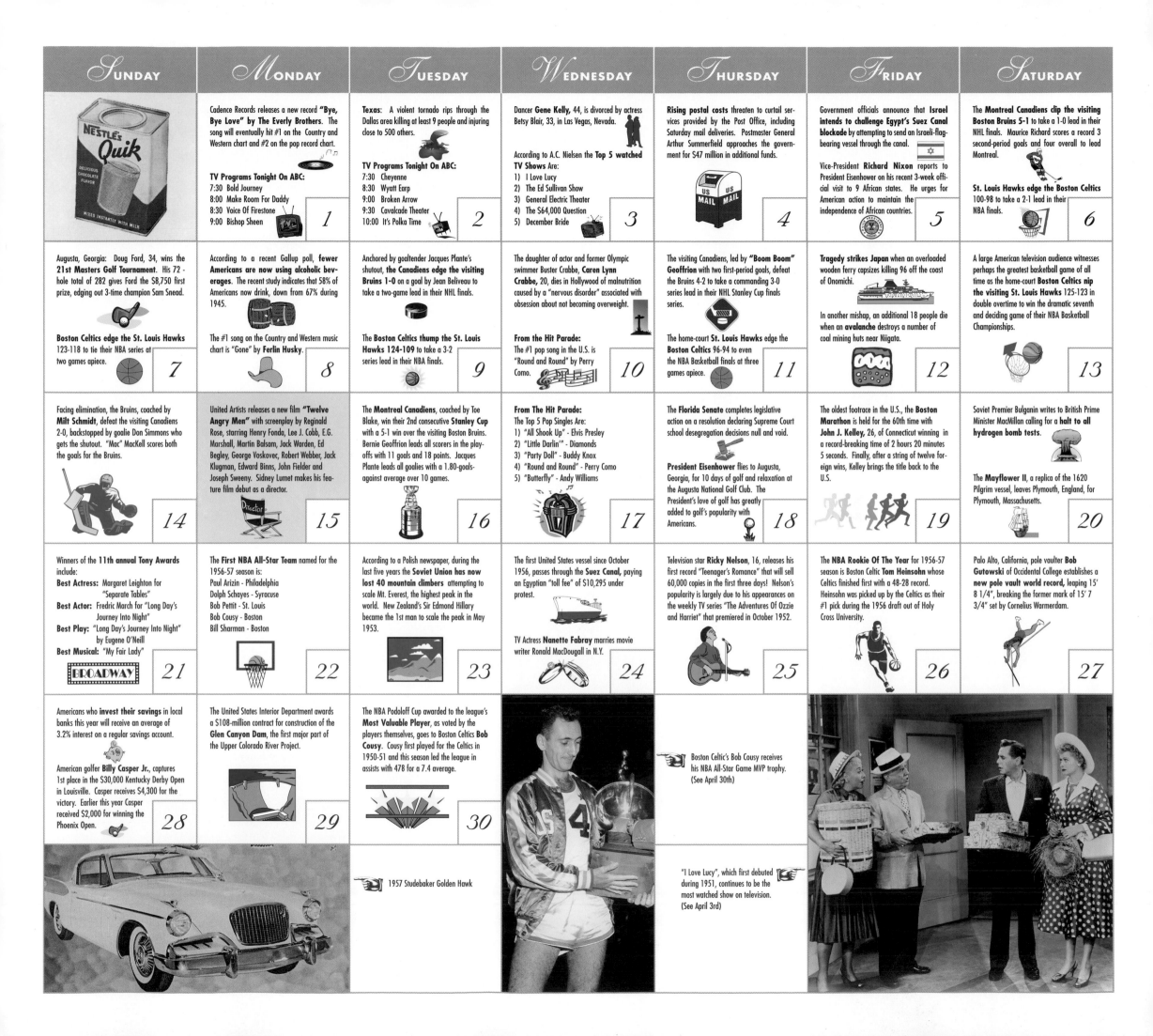

1957 Studebaker Golden Hawk

"I Love Lucy", which first debuted during 1951, continues to be the most watched show on television. (See April 3rd)

M A Y

1957

Driver Sam Hanks celebrates his victory at the Indianapolis 500.

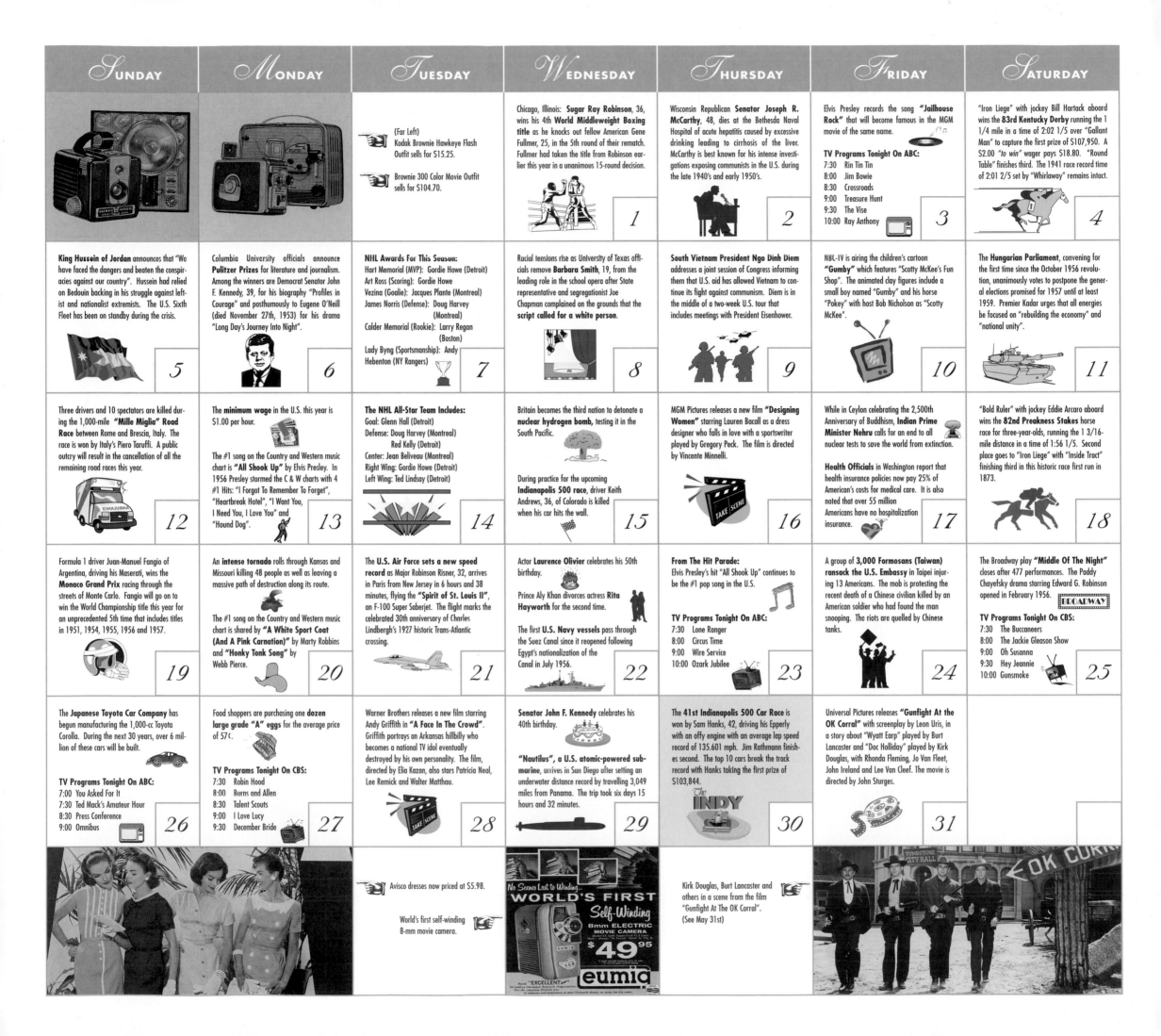

Sunday	Monday	Tuesday	Wednesday	Thursday	Friday	Saturday

Tuesday (Far Left)
Kodak Brownie Hawkeye Flash Outfit sells for $15.25.

Brownie 300 Color Movie Outfit sells for $104.70.

Wednesday 1
Chicago, Illinois: **Sugar Ray Robinson**, 36, wins his 4th **World Middleweight Boxing title** as he knocks out fellow American Gene Fullmer, 25, in the 5th round of their rematch. Fullmer had taken the title from Robinson earlier this year in a unanimous 15-round decision.

Thursday 2
Wisconsin Republican **Senator Joseph R. McCarthy**, 48, dies at the Bethesda Naval Hospital of acute hepatitis caused by excessive drinking leading to cirrhosis of the liver. McCarthy is best known for his intense investigations exposing communists in the U.S. during the late 1940's and early 1950's.

Friday 3
Elvis Presley records the song **"Jailhouse Rock"** that will become famous in the MGM movie of the same name.

TV Programs Tonight On ABC:
7:30   Rin Tin Tin
8:00   Jim Bowie
8:30   Crossroads
9:00   Treasure Hunt
9:30   The Vise
10:00 Ray Anthony

Saturday 4
"Iron Liege" with jockey Bill Hartack aboard wins the **83rd Kentucky Derby** running the 1 1/4 mile in a time of 2:02 1/5 over "Gallant Man" to capture the first prize of $107,950. A $2.00 "to win" wager pays $18.80. "Round Table" finishes third. The 1941 race record time of 2:01 2/5 set by "Whirlaway" remains intact.

Sunday 5
King Hussein of Jordan announces that "We have faced the dangers and beaten the conspiracies against our country". Hussein had relied on Bedouin backing in his struggle against leftist and nationalist extremists. The U.S. Sixth Fleet has been on standby during the crisis.

Monday 6
Columbia University officials announce **Pulitzer Prizes** for literature and journalism. Among the winners are Democrat Senator John F. Kennedy, 39, for his biography "Profiles in Courage" and posthumously to Eugene O'Neill (died November 27th, 1953) for his drama "Long Day's Journey Into Night".

Tuesday 7
NHL Awards For This Season:
Hart Memorial (MVP): Gordie Howe (Detroit)
Art Ross (Scoring): Gordie Howe
Vezina (Goalie): Jacques Plante (Montreal)
James Norris (Defense): Doug Harvey (Montreal)
Calder Memorial (Rookie): Larry Regan (Boston)
Lady Byng (Sportsmanship): Andy Hebenton (NY Rangers)

Wednesday 8
Racial tensions rise as University of Texas officials remove **Barbara Smith**, 19, from the leading role in the school opera after State representative and segregationist Joe Chapman complained on the grounds that the **script called for a white person.**

Thursday 9
South Vietnam President Ngo Dinh Diem addresses a joint session of Congress informing them that U.S. aid has allowed Vietnam to continue its fight against communism. Diem is in the middle of a two-week U.S. tour that includes meetings with President Eisenhower.

Friday 10
NBC-IV is airing the children's cartoon **"Gumby"** which features "Scotty McKee's Fun Shop". The animated clay figures include a small boy named "Gumby" and his horse "Pokey" with host Bob Nicholson as "Scotty McKee".

Saturday 11
The **Hungarian Parliament**, convening for the first time since the October 1956 revolution, unanimously votes to postpone the general elections promised for 1957 until at least 1959. Premier Kadar urges that all energies be focused on "rebuilding the economy" and "national unity".

Sunday 12
Three drivers and 10 spectators are killed during the 1,000-mile **"Mille Miglia" Road Race** between Rome and Brescia, Italy. The race is won by Italy's Piero Taruffi. A public outcry will result in the cancellation of all the remaining road races this year.

Monday 13
The **minimum wage** in the U.S. this year is $1.00 per hour.

The #1 song on the Country and Western music chart is **"All Shook Up"** by Elvis Presley. In 1956 Presley stormed the C & W charts with 4 #1 Hits: "I Forgot To Remember To Forget", "Heartbreak Hotel", "I Want You, I Need You, I Love You" and "Hound Dog".

Tuesday 14
The NHL All-Star Team Includes:
Goal: Glenn Hall (Detroit)
Defense: Doug Harvey (Montreal)
Red Kelly (Detroit)
Center: Jean Beliveau (Montreal)
Right Wing: Gordie Howe (Detroit)
Left Wing: Ted Lindsay (Detroit)

Wednesday 15
Britain becomes the third nation to detonate a **nuclear hydrogen bomb**, testing it in the South Pacific.

During practice for the upcoming Indianapolis 500 race, driver Keith Andrews, 36, of Colorado is killed when his car hits the wall.

Thursday 16
MGM Pictures releases a new film **"Designing Women"** starring Lauren Bacall as a dress designer who falls in love with a sportswriter played by Gregory Peck. The film is directed by Vincente Minnelli.

Friday 17
While in Ceylon celebrating the 2,500th Anniversary of Buddhism, **Indian Prime Minister Nehru** calls for an end to all nuclear tests to save the world from extinction.

Health Officials in Washington report that health insurance policies now pay 25% of American's costs for medical care. It is also noted that over 55 million Americans have no hospitalization insurance.

Saturday 18
"Bold Ruler" with jockey Eddie Arcaro aboard wins the **82nd Preakness Stakes** horse race for three-year-olds, running the 1 3/16-mile distance in a time of 1:56 1/5. Second place goes to "Iron Liege" with "Inside Tract" finishing third in this historic race first run in 1873.

Sunday 19
Formula 1 driver Juan-Manuel Fangio of Argentina, driving his Maserati, wins the **Monaco Grand Prix** racing through the streets of Monte Carlo. Fangio will go on to win the World Championship title this year for an unprecedented 5th time that includes titles in 1951, 1954, 1955, 1956 and 1957.

Monday 20
An intense tornado rolls through Kansas and Missouri killing 48 people as well as leaving a massive path of destruction along its route.

The #1 song on the Country and Western music chart is shared by **"A White Sport Coat (And A Pink Carnation)"** by Marty Robbins and **"Honky Tonk Song"** by Webb Pierce.

Tuesday 21
The **U.S. Air Force sets a new speed record** as Major Robinson Risner, 32, arrives in Paris from New Jersey in 6 hours and 38 minutes, flying the **"Spirit of St. Louis II"**, an F-100 Super Saberjet. The flight marks the celebrated 30th anniversary of Charles Lindbergh's 1927 historic Trans-Atlantic crossing.

Wednesday 22
Actor **Laurence Olivier** celebrates his 50th birthday.

Prince Aly Khan divorces actress **Rita Hayworth** for the second time.

The first **U.S. Navy vessels** pass through the Suez Canal since it reopened following Egypt's nationalization of the Canal in July 1956.

Thursday 23
From The Hit Parade:
Elvis Presley's hit "All Shook Up" continues to be the #1 pop song in the U.S.

TV Programs Tonight On ABC:
7:30   Lone Ranger
8:00   Circus Time
9:00   Wire Service
10:00 Ozark Jubilee

Friday 24
A group of **3,000 Formosans (Taiwan)** ransack the U.S. Embassy in Taipei injuring 13 Americans. The mob is protesting the recent death of a Chinese civilian killed by an American soldier who had found the man snooping. The riots are quelled by Chinese tanks.

Saturday 25
The Broadway play **"Middle Of The Night"** closes after 477 performances. The Paddy Chayefsky drama starring Edward G. Robinson opened in February 1956.

TV Programs Tonight On CBS:
7:30   The Buccaneers
8:00   The Jackie Gleason Show
9:00   Oh Susanna
9:30   Hey Jeannie
10:00 Gunsmoke

Sunday 26
The **Japanese Toyota Car Company** has begun manufacturing the 1,000-cc Toyota Corolla. During the next 30 years, over 6 million of these cars will be built.

TV Programs Tonight On ABC:
7:00   You Asked For It
7:30   Ted Mack's Amateur Hour
8:30   Press Conference
9:00   Omnibus

Monday 27
Food shoppers are purchasing one **dozen large grade "A" eggs** for the average price of 57¢.

TV Programs Tonight On CBS:
7:30   Robin Hood
8:00   Burns and Allen
8:30   Talent Scouts
9:00   I Love Lucy
9:30   December Bride

Tuesday 28
Warner Brothers releases a new film starring Andy Griffith in **"A Face In The Crowd"**. Griffith portrays an Arkansas hillbilly who becomes a national TV idol eventually destroyed by his own personality. The film, directed by Elia Kazan, also stars Patricia Neal, Lee Remick and Walter Matthau.

Wednesday 29
Senator **John F. Kennedy** celebrates his 40th birthday.

"Nautilus", a U.S. atomic-powered submarine, arrives in San Diego after setting an underwater distance record by travelling 3,049 miles from Panama. The trip took six days 15 hours and 32 minutes.

Thursday 30
The **41st Indianapolis 500 Car Race** is won by Sam Hanks, 42, driving his Epperly with an offy engine with an average lap speed record of 135.601 mph. Jim Rathmann finishes second. The top 10 cars break the track record with Hanks taking the first prize of $103,844.

Friday 31
Universal Pictures releases **"Gunfight At the OK Corral"** with screenplay by Leon Uris, in a story about "Wyatt Earp" played by Burt Lancaster and "Doc Holliday" played by Kirk Douglas, with Rhonda Fleming, Jo Van Fleet, John Ireland and Lee Van Cleef. The movie is directed by John Sturges.

UCLA's Don Bowden becomes the first American to break the 4-minute mile.

Sunday	Monday	Tuesday	Wednesday	Thursday	Friday	Saturday
	☞ Dick Mayer and Cary Middlecoff are tied at 72 holes of regulation play at the U.S. Open. (See June 14th)	**Love is the Thing** THE voice of NAT KING COLE	☞ Nat King Cole tops the Album Chart with his hit LP "Love Is The Thing". (See June 24th) 1957 Pontiac Superchief ☞			**Don Bowden**, 20, of UCLA becomes the "first American" to officially run a mile in under four minutes with a time of 3:58.7 at Berkeley, California. Sweden's Sven Davidson and England's Shirley Bloomer capture the singles titles at the **French Tennis Championships**. **1**
CBS airs a **"Face The Nation"** TV broadcast in which Soviet C.P. First Secretary Nikita Khrushchev is interviewed by American correspondents (filmed unrehearsed in Moscow 5 days ago). Khrushchev predicts that "your grandchildren will live under socialism". **2**	The **U.S. Supreme Court** rules 7-1 that the Government must drop criminal prosecution in cases where they refuse to allow the accused to examine secret FBI files. Judge Tom Clark, the former Attorney General is the only member who did not support the ruling. **3**	Defending **World Baseball Champion New York Yankee** stars Mickey Mantle, Yogi Berra, Whitey Ford, Hank Bauer and Billy Martin are each fined $1,000 for recently breaking curfew when they were out celebrating Martin's birthday. **4**	In an attempt to reduce the population growth rate, the Chinese Government legalizes **abortions** and encourages contraceptive **birth control measures**. It is estimated that there are now close to 635 million Chinese, increasing by 18 million each year. **5**	Narcotics expert Dr. Herbert Berger suggests that an **investigation be launched into the use of stimulative drugs by athletes** to improve their performances. It is Berger's opinion that a mile could not be run in under 4 minutes without stimulants such as amphetamines. **6**	Actor **Dean Martin** celebrates his 40th birthday. World Lightweight Boxing Champion **Archie Moore** is suspended by the National Boxing Association when he fails to appear for a scheduled title match with Tony Anthony in Detroit. **7**	The historic 89th running of Canada's prestigious horse racing event, **The Queen's Plate**, takes place in Toronto. North America's oldest continuously run stakes race is won by "Lyford Cay", a 3-year-old bay gelding with jockey Avelino Gomez aboard. "Lyford Cay's" owner E.P. Taylor, collects a $26,070 purse. "Inside Tract" places second with "Bold Ruler" finishing third. **8**
From The Hit Parade: The #1 hit single in the United Kingdom this week is Johnnie Ray's **"Yes, Tonight, Josephine"**. Ray's hit replaces Andy William's "Butterfly" at the top of the charts. Golfer **Arnold Palmer**, 27, captures the Rubber City Open in Akron, Ohio, to win $2,800. **9**	A **national election in Canada** results in a major political upset as the Liberal Party, who has led Canada for the last 22 years, is defeated by the Conservatives led by John Diefenbaker. Prime Minister Louis St. Laurent, 75, will reluctantly resign one week from now. **10**	A **railroad accident** occurs in Vroman, Colorado, as 12 farm laborers are killed when their truck is hit by a Sante Fe freight train. The first test of an **Atlas Intercontinental Missile** ends in failure as it explodes shortly after takeoff from Cape Canaveral, Florida. **11**	Jimmy Dorsey, 53, a "Big Band Leader" during the last 25 years, dies of lung cancer in New York. Dorsey's partner and brother Tommy died in November 1956 after choking to death in his sleep. **"Mayflower II"** arrives in Plymouth, Massachusetts. **12**	Responding to Dr. Herbert Berger, **track and field milers** Roger Bannister, Don Bowden and Ron Delaney issue strong denials that stimulant drugs helped them break the 4-minute barrier. **13**	Cary Middlecoff birdies the final hole to force an 18-hole play-off against Dick Mayer, 34, at the **57th U.S. Open Golf Tournament** at the Inverness Golf Club in Toledo, Ohio. The play-off will turn out to be a rout as Mayer will win tomorrow by 7 strokes (72-79) to take the $7,200 first prize. **14**	"Gallant Man" with jockey Willie Shoemaker wins the historic **Belmont Stakes Horse Race**, running the 1 1/2-mile distance in a record time of 2:26 3/5. Yale wins the 92nd Rowing Race against Harvard in New London, Connecticut. Harvard now leads the series 47-45. **15**
The Gillette Company has introduced the **first adjustable safety razor**. King Gillette had introduced the immensely successful first safety razor with replaceable blades during 1903. Now a multi-million-dollar worldwide corporation, Gillette continues to introduce new shaving advancements for the world's men. **16**	In an historic ruling, the **U.S. Supreme Court** rules 6-1 to free 5 California communists convicted under the Smith Act. New trials are ordered for 9 others. Justices Whittaker and Brennan did not participate in the case. **17**	NFL Green Bay Packer football player **Rudy Schoendorf**, 21, is shot and killed during an incident at a Bowling Green, Ohio, tavern. New York Giant linesman Norman Mooney, 22, is also injured during the shooting. **18**	The Walt Disney film **"Johnny Tremain"** is released to theaters across the nation. The adaptation of the Esther Forbes novel stars Hal Stalmaster as "Johnny Tremain", a young boy who gets caught up in the revolutionary war. **19**	A 5'10" professional weight lifter from Georgia, **Paul Anderson**, successfully lifts 6,270 lbs off the ground setting a new weight record in an incredible display of strength. **20**	Track star **Glenn Davis** of Ohio State sets a new world record of 50.9 seconds in the 440-yard hurdles at the National AAU meet in Dayton, Ohio. **21**	Two successful plays close after long runs on Broadway. **"Dairy Of Anne Frank"** brings down the final curtain following 720 performances while **"Inherit The Wind"** closes after 803 performances. Both plays 1st appeared in mid-1955. **BROADWAY** **22**
The **Automobile Club de L'Ouest Le Mans** 24-hour endurance race, run on a 8.364-mile circuit, is won by Scottish teammates Flockhart & Bueb driving their Jaguar. Their average speed is 113.845 mph. Of the 54 cars that started, only 20 finished in the 24-hour Le Mans that first began in 1923. **23**	**From The Hit Parade:** The #1 U.S. LP for the sixth straight week is Nat King Cole's album **"Love Is The Thing"**. The Supreme Court rules that **obscenity** is not protected by the Constitutional guarantee of free speech. **24**	Americans study a recent **American Cancer Society report** to the AMA that "cigarette smoking has an extremely high association with gastric ulcers, aortic aneurysm, and cancer of the lung, larynx and bladder". Despite the report, more Americans now smoke than ever before. **25**	Paramount Pictures releases the film **"Beau James"** starring Bob Hope as former N.Y. Mayor "Jimmy Walker" with co-stars Vera Miles, Paul Douglas, Darren McGavin and Alexis Smith. The movie is narrated by Walter Winchell. **ADMIT ONE** **26**	**Hurricane Audrey** devastates Cameron, Louisiana, as well as surrounding areas. The storm, supported by 110-mph winds and a 20-foot tidal wave, lashes Louisiana and Texas taking at least 550 lives. President Eisenhower will declare the affected counties a disaster area. **27**	**From The Hit Parade:** The #1 pop single continues to be Pat Boone's "Love Letters In The Sand". The NAACP recognizes civil rights leader **Martin Luther King Jr.** by awarding him the "Spingarn Award" for high achievement. **28**	American Betsy Rawls is declared the winner of this year's **Women's U.S. Golf Open** after the apparent winner Jacqueline Pung, 35, of San Francisco is disqualified for submitting an incorrect score card. Rawls wins the event on the Winged Foot Golf & Country Club in Mamaroneck, N.Y. The members of the golf club raise $2,500 however to give to Pung as a "consolation fund". **29**
The book by author Hank Ketcham's, **"Dennis The Menace: Household Hurricane"** is being read around the nation. "Dennis the Menace" comic strips, along with this book, will lead to a popular new TV series that will premiere 2 years from now starring Jay North. **30**		☞ 1957 Corvette	U.S. Open Golf Champion Betsy Rawls ☞ accepts her trophy much to the dismay of disqualified opponent Jacqueline Pung (seated in bottom left). (See June 29th)			

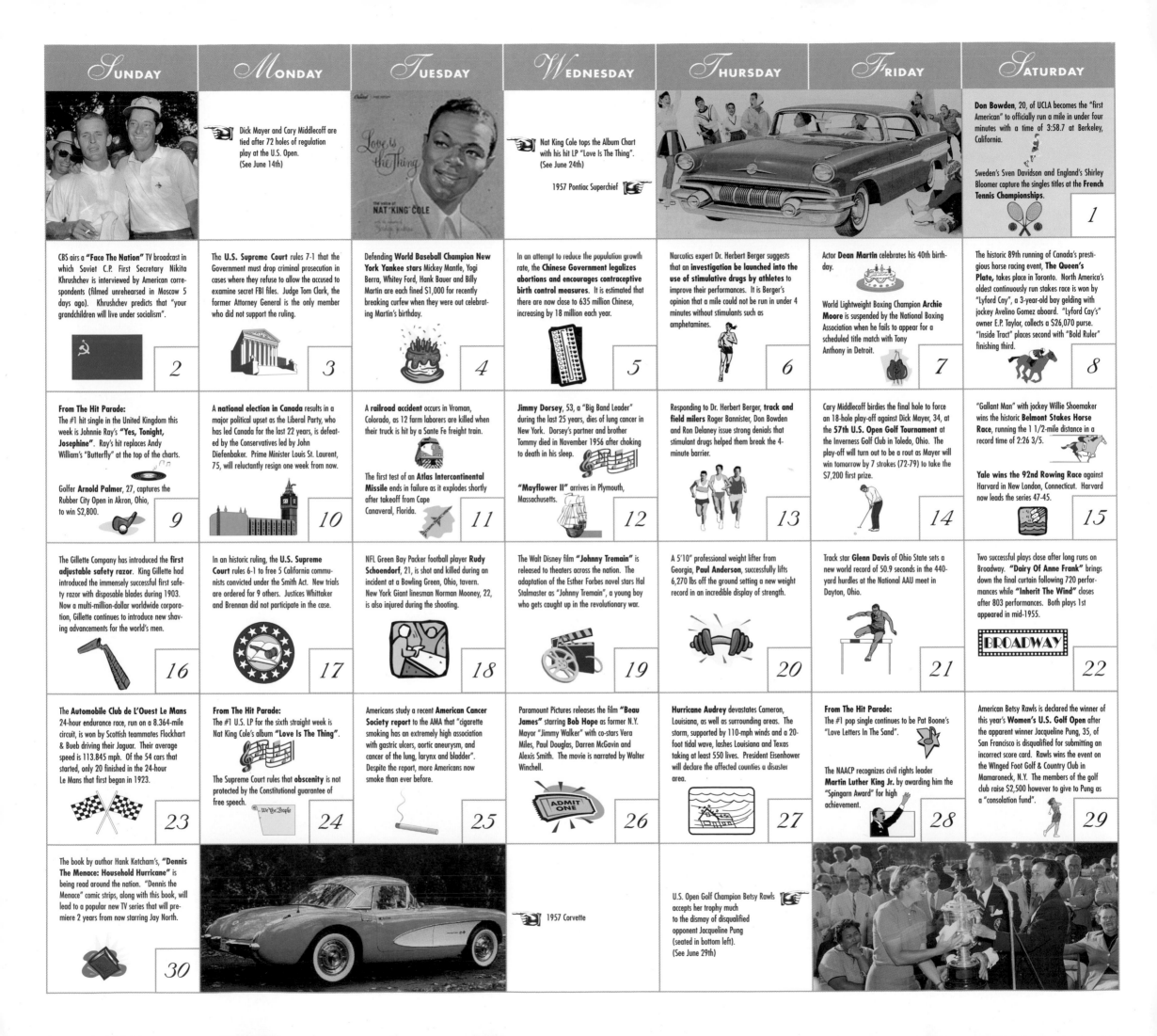

J U L Y

1957

Alan Freed hosts the rock and roll television show "The Big Beat".

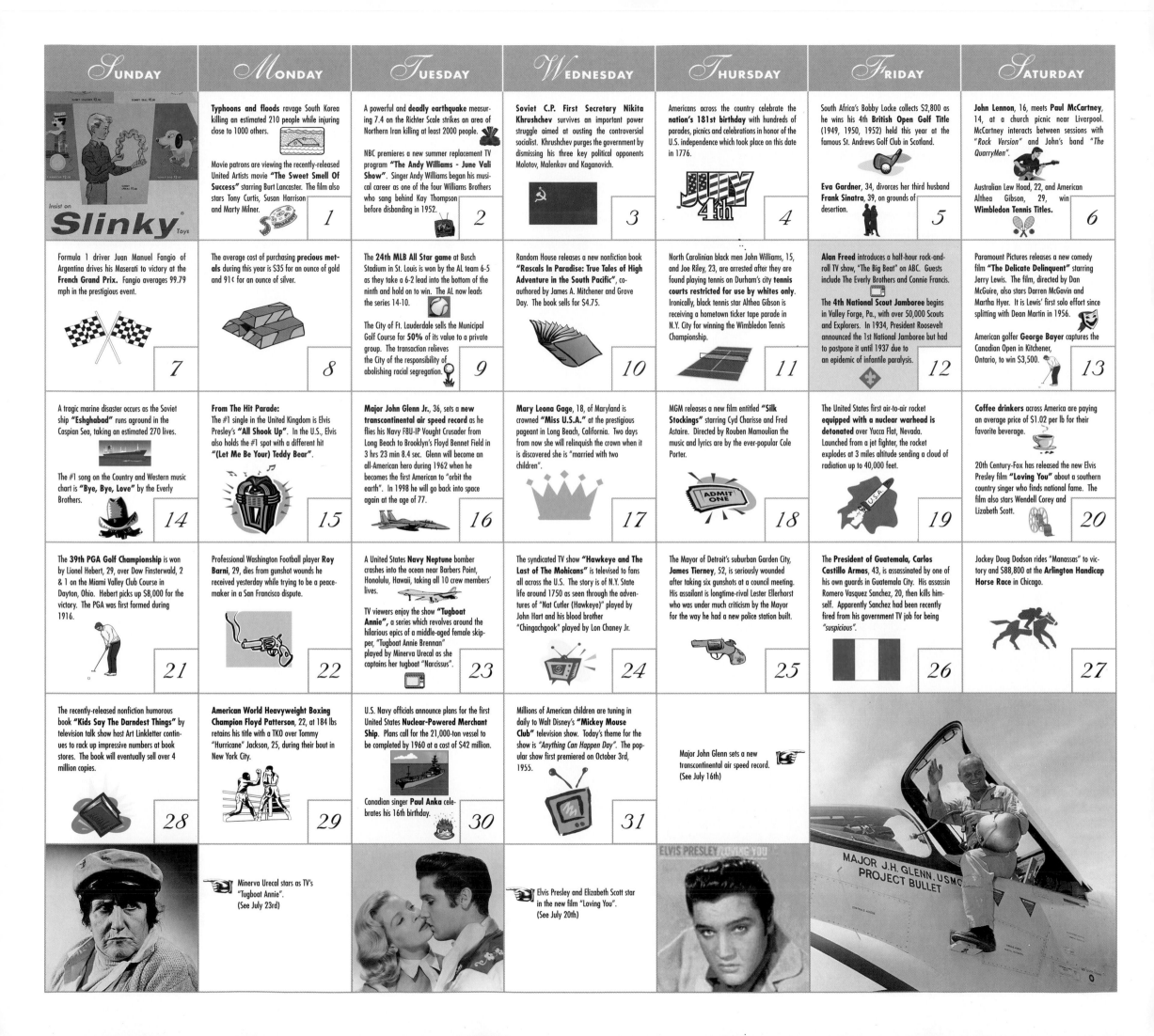

Sunday	Monday	Tuesday	Wednesday	Thursday	Friday	Saturday
Insist on **Slinky** Toys	**Typhoons and floods** ravage South Korea killing an estimated 210 people while injuring close to 1000 others. / Movie patrons are viewing the recently-released United Artists movie **"The Sweet Smell Of Success"** starring Burt Lancaster. The film also stars Tony Curtis, Susan Harrison and Marty Milner. **1**	A powerful and **deadly earthquake** measuring 7.4 on the Richter Scale strikes an area of Northern Iran killing at least 2000 people. / NBC premieres a new summer replacement TV program **"The Andy Williams - June Vali Show"**. Singer Andy Williams began his musical career as one of the four Williams Brothers who sang behind Kay Thompson before disbanding in 1952. **2**	Soviet C.P. First Secretary Nikita Khrushchev survives an important power struggle aimed at ousting the controversial socialist. Khrushchev purges the government by dismissing his three key political opponents Molotov, Malenkov and Kaganovich. **3**	Americans across the country celebrate the **nation's 181st birthday** with hundreds of parades, picnics and celebrations in honor of the U.S. independence which took place on this date in 1776. **4**	South Africa's Bobby Locke collects $2,800 as he wins his 4th **British Open Golf Title** (1949, 1950, 1952) held this year at the famous St. Andrews Golf Club in Scotland. / **Eva Gardner**, 34, divorces her third husband **Frank Sinatra**, 39, on grounds of desertion. **5**	**John Lennon**, 16, meets **Paul McCartney**, 14, at a church picnic near Liverpool. McCartney interacts between sessions with "Rock Version" and John's band "The QuarryMen". / Australian Lew Hood, 22, and American Althea Gibson, 29, win **Wimbledon Tennis Titles**. **6**
Formula 1 driver Juan Manuel Fangio of Argentina drives his Maserati to victory at the **French Grand Prix**. Fangio averages 99.79 mph in the prestigious event. **7**	The average cost of purchasing **precious metals** during this year is $35 for an ounce of gold and 91¢ for an ounce of silver. **8**	The 24th MLB All Star game at Busch Stadium in St. Louis is won by the AL team 6-5 as they take a 6-2 lead into the bottom of the ninth and hold on to win. The AL now leads the series 14-10. / The City of Ft. Lauderdale sells the Municipal Golf Course for **50%** of its value to a private group. The transaction relieves the City of the responsibility of abolishing racial segregation. **9**	Random House releases a new nonfiction book **"Rascals In Paradise: True Tales of High Adventure in the South Pacific"**, co-authored by James A. Mitchener and Grove Day. The book sells for $4.75. **10**	North Carolinian black men John Williams, 15, and Joe Riley, 23, are arrested after they are found playing tennis on Durham's city **tennis courts restricted for use by whites only**. Ironically, black tennis star Althea Gibson is receiving a hometown ticker tape parade in N.Y. City for winning the Wimbledon Tennis Championship. **11**	**Alan Freed** introduces a half-hour rock-and-roll TV show, "The Big Beat" on ABC. Guests include The Everly Brothers and Connie Francis. / The **4th National Scout Jamboree** begins in Valley Forge, Pa., with over 50,000 Scouts and Explorers. In 1934, President Roosevelt announced the 1st National Jamboree but had to postpone it until 1937 due to an epidemic of infantile paralysis. **12**	American golfer George Bayer captures the Canadian Open in Kitchener, Ontario, to win $3,500. **13**
A tragic marine disaster occurs as the Soviet ship **"Eshghabad"** runs aground in the Caspian Sea, taking an estimated 270 lives. / The #1 song on the Country and Western music chart is "Bye, Bye, Love" by the Everly Brothers. **14**	From The Hit Parade: The #1 single in the United Kingdom is Elvis Presley's **"All Shook Up"**. In the U.S., Elvis also holds the #1 spot with a different hit **"(Let Me Be Your) Teddy Bear"**. **15**	**Major John Glenn Jr.**, 36, sets a **new transcontinental air speed record** as he flies his Navy F8U-IP Vought Crusader from Long Beach to Brooklyn's Floyd Bennet Field in 3 hrs 23 min 8.4 sec. Glenn will become an all-American hero during 1962 when he becomes the first American to "orbit the earth". In 1998 he will go back into space again at the age of 77. **16**	**Mary Leona Gage**, 18, of Maryland is crowned **"Miss U.S.A."** at the prestigious pageant in Long Beach, California. Two days from now she will relinquish the crown when it is discovered she is "married with two children". **17**	MGM releases a new film entitled **"Silk Stockings"** starring Cyd Charisse and Fred Astaire. Directed by Rouben Mamoulian the music and lyrics are by the ever-popular Cole Porter. **18**	The United States first air-to-air rocket equipped with a **nuclear warhead is detonated** over Yucca Flat, Nevada. Launched from a jet fighter, the rocket explodes at 3 miles altitude sending a cloud of radiation up to 40,000 feet. **19**	**Coffee drinkers** across America are paying an average price of $1.02 per lb for their favorite beverage. / 20th Century-Fox has released the new Elvis Presley film **"Loving You"** about a southern country singer who finds national fame. The film also stars Wendell Corey and Lizabeth Scott. **20**
The 39th PGA Golf Championship is won by Lionel Hebert, 29, over Dow Finsterwald, 2 & 1 on the Miami Valley Club Course in Dayton, Ohio. Hebert picks up $8,000 for the victory. The PGA was first formed during 1916. **21**	Professional Washington Football player **Roy Barni**, 29, dies from gunshot wounds he received yesterday while trying to be a peacemaker in a San Francisco dispute. **22**	A United States **Navy Neptune** bomber crashes into the ocean near Barbers Point, Honolulu, Hawaii, taking all 10 crew members' lives. / TV viewers enjoy the show **"Tugboat Annie"**, a series which revolves around the hilarious epics of a middle-aged female skipper, "Tugboat Annie Brennan" played by Minerva Urecal as she captains her tugboat "Narcissus". **23**	The syndicated TV show **"Hawkeye and The Last of The Mohicans"** is televised to fans all across the U.S. The story is of N.Y. State life around 1750 as seen through the adventures of "Nat Cutler (Hawkeye)" played by John Hart and his blood brother "Chingachgook" played by Lon Chaney Jr. **24**	The Mayor of Detroit's suburban Garden City, **James Tierney**, 52, is seriously wounded after taking six gunshots at a council meeting. His assailant is longtime-rival Lester Ellerhorst who was under much criticism by the Mayor for the way he had a new police station built. **25**	The **President of Guatemala, Carlos Castillo Armas**, 43, is assassinated by one of his own guards in Guatemala City. His assassin Romero Vasquez Sanchez, 20, then kills himself. Apparently Sanchez had been recently fired from his government TV job for being "suspicious". **26**	Jockey Doug Dodson rides "Manassas" to victory and $88,800 at the **Arlington Handicap Horse Race** in Chicago. **27**
The recently-released nonfiction humorous book **"Kids Say The Darndest Things"** by television talk show host Art Linkletter continues to rack up impressive numbers at book stores. The book will eventually sell over 4 million copies. **28**	**American World Heavyweight Boxing Champion Floyd Patterson**, 22, at 184 lbs retains his title with a TKO over Tommy "Hurricane" Jackson, 25, during their bout in New York City. **29**	U.S. Navy officials announce plans for the first United States **Nuclear-Powered Merchant Ship**. Plans call for the 21,000-ton vessel to be completed by 1960 at a cost of $42 million. / Canadian singer **Paul Anka** celebrates his 16th birthday. **30**	Millions of American children are tuning in daily to Walt Disney's **"Mickey Mouse Club"** television show. Today's theme for the show is "Anything Can Happen Day". The popular show first premiered on October 3rd, 1955. **31**	Major John Glenn sets a new transcontinental air speed record. (See July 16th)		

Minerva Urecal stars as TV's "Tugboat Annie". (See July 23rd)

Elvis Presley and Elizabeth Scott star in the new film "Loving You". (See July 20th)

ELVIS PRESLEY LOVING YOU

MAJOR J.H. GLENN, USMC PROJECT BULLET

Dick Clark hosts the new TV show "American Bandstand".

Sunday	Monday	Tuesday	Wednesday	Thursday	Friday	Saturday

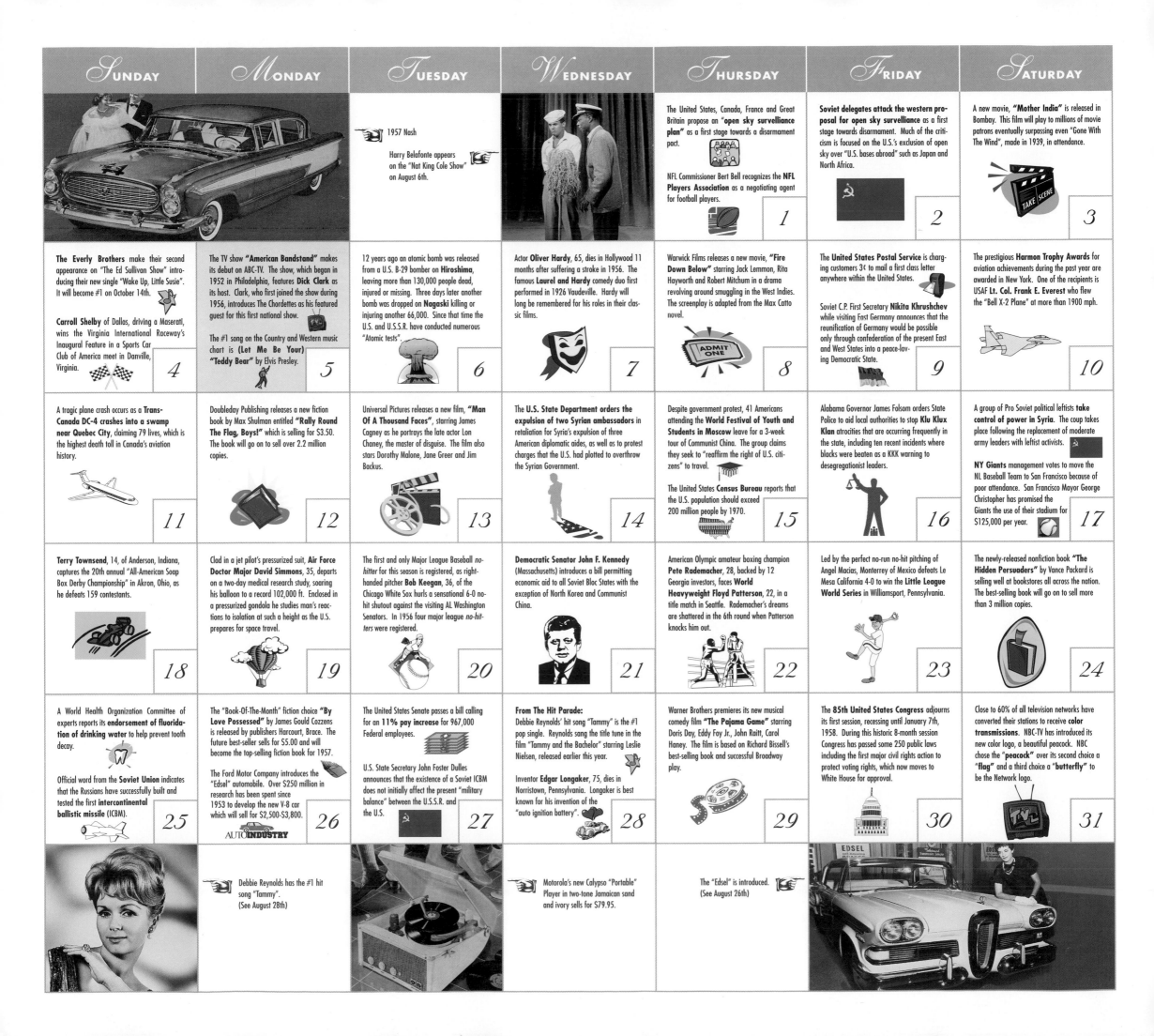

Tuesday: 1957 Nash

Harry Belafonte appears on the "Nat King Cole Show" on August 6th.

Thursday 1: The United States, Canada, France and Great Britain propose an **"open sky survelliance plan"** as a first stage towards a disarmament pact.

NFL Commissioner Bert Bell recognizes the **NFL Players Association** as a negotiating agent for football players.

Friday 2: **Soviet delegates attack the western proposal for open sky survelliance** as a first stage towards disarmament. Much of the criticism is focused on the U.S.'s exclusion of open sky over "U.S. bases abroad" such as Japan and North Africa.

Saturday 3: A new movie, **"Mother India"** is released in Bombay. This film will play to millions of movie patrons eventually surpassing even "Gone With The Wind", made in 1939, in attendance.

Sunday 4: The **Everly Brothers** make their second appearance on "The Ed Sullivan Show" introducing their new single "Wake Up, Little Susie". It will become #1 on October 14th.

Carroll Shelby of Dallas, driving a Maserati, wins the Virginia International Raceway's Inaugural Feature in a Sports Car Club of America meet in Danville, Virginia.

Monday 5: The TV show **"American Bandstand"** makes its debut on ABC-TV. The show, which began in 1952 in Philadelphia, features **Dick Clark** as its host. Clark, who first joined the show during 1956, introduces The Chordettes as his featured guest for this first national show.

The #1 song on the Country and Western music chart is **(Let Me Be Your) "Teddy Bear"** by Elvis Presley.

Tuesday 6: 12 years ago an atomic bomb was released from a U.S. B-29 bomber on **Hiroshima**, leaving more than 130,000 people dead, injured or missing. Three days later another bomb was dropped on **Nagaski** killing or injuring another 66,000. Since that time the U.S. and U.S.S.R. have conducted numerous "Atomic tests".

Wednesday 7: Actor **Oliver Hardy**, 65, dies in Hollywood 11 months after suffering a stroke in 1956. The famous **Laurel and Hardy** comedy duo first performed in 1926 Vaudeville. Hardy will long be remembered for his roles in their classic films.

Thursday 8: Warwick Films releases a new movie, **"Fire Down Below"** starring Jack Lemmon, Rita Hayworth and Robert Mitchum in a drama revolving around smuggling in the West Indies. The screenplay is adapted from the Max Catto novel.

Friday 9: The **United States Postal Service** is charging customers 3¢ to mail a first class letter anywhere within the United States.

Soviet C.P. First Secretary **Nikita Khrushchev** while visiting East Germany announces that the reunification of Germany would be possible only through confederation of the present East and West States into a peace-loving Democratic State.

Saturday 10: The prestigious **Harmon Trophy Awards** for aviation achievements during the past year are awarded in New York. One of the recipients is USAF **Lt. Col. Frank E. Everest** who flew the "Bell X-2 Plane" at more than 1900 mph.

Sunday 11: A tragic plane crash occurs as a **Trans-Canada DC-4 crashes into a swamp near Quebec City**, claiming 79 lives, which is the highest death toll in Canada's aviation history.

Monday 12: Doubleday Publishing releases a new fiction book by Max Shulman entitled **"Rally Round The Flag, Boys!"** which is selling for $3.50. The book will go on to sell over 2.2 million copies.

Tuesday 13: Universal Pictures releases a new film, **"Man Of A Thousand Faces"**, starring James Cagney as he portrays the late actor Lon Chaney, the master of disguise. The film also stars Dorothy Malone, Jane Greer and Jim Backus.

Wednesday 14: The **U.S. State Department** orders the expulsion of two Syrian ambassadors in retaliation for Syria's expulsion of three American diplomatic aides, as well as to protest charges that the U.S. had plotted to overthrow the Syrian Government.

Thursday 15: Despite government protest, 41 Americans attending the **World Festival of Youth and Students in Moscow** leave for a 3-week tour of Communist China. The group claims they seek to "reaffirm the right of U.S. citizens" to travel.

The United States **Census Bureau** reports that the U.S. population should exceed 200 million people by 1970.

Friday 16: Alabama Governor James Folsom orders State Police to aid local authorities to stop **Klu Klux Klan** atrocities that are occurring frequently in the state, including ten recent incidents where blacks were beaten as a KKK warning to desegregationist leaders.

Saturday 17: A group of Pro Soviet political leftists **take control of power in Syria**. The coup takes place following the replacement of moderate army leaders with leftist activists.

NY Giants management votes to move the NL Baseball Team to San Francisco because of poor attendance. San Francisco Mayor George Christopher has promised the Giants the use of their stadium for $125,000 per year.

Sunday 18: **Terry Townsend**, 14, of Anderson, Indiana, captures the 20th annual "All-American Soap Box Derby Championship" in Akron, Ohio, as he defeats 159 contestants.

Monday 19: Clad in a jet pilot's pressurized suit, **Air Force Doctor Major David Simmons**, 35, departs on a two-day medical research study, soaring his balloon to a record 102,000 ft. Enclosed in a pressurized gondola he studies man's reactions to isolation at such a height as the U.S. prepares for space travel.

Tuesday 20: The first and only Major League Baseball *no-hitter* for this season is registered, as right-handed pitcher **Bob Keegan**, 36, of the Chicago White Sox hurls a sensational 6-0 no-hit shutout against the visiting AL Washington Senators. In 1956 four major league *no-hitters* were registered.

Wednesday 21: Democratic Senator **John F. Kennedy** (Massachusetts) introduces a bill permitting economic aid to all Soviet Bloc States with the exception of North Korea and Communist China.

Thursday 22: American Olympic amateur boxing champion **Pete Rademacher**, 28, backed by 12 Georgia investors, faces **World Heavyweight Floyd Patterson**, 22, in a title match in Seattle. Rademacher's dreams are shattered in the 6th round when Patterson knocks him out.

Friday 23: Led by the perfect no-run no-hit pitching of Angel Macias, Monterrey of Mexico defeats Le Mesa California 4-0 to win the **Little League World Series** in Williamsport, Pennsylvania.

Saturday 24: The newly-released nonfiction book **"The Hidden Persuaders"** by Vance Packard is selling well at bookstores all across the nation. The best-selling book will go on to sell more than 3 million copies.

Sunday 25: A World Health Organization Committee of experts reports its **endorsement of fluoridation of drinking water** to help prevent tooth decay.

Official word from the **Soviet Union** indicates that the Russians have successfully built and tested the first **intercontinental ballistic missile (ICBM)**.

Monday 26: The "Book-Of-The-Month" fiction choice **"By Love Possessed"** by James Gould Cozzens is released by publishers Harcourt, Brace. The future best-seller sells for $5.00 and will become the top-selling fiction book for 1957.

The Ford Motor Company introduces the "Edsel" automobile. Over $250 million in research has been spent since 1953 to develop the new V-8 car which will sell for $2,500-$3,800.

AUTO**INDUSTRY**

Tuesday 27: The United States Senate passes a bill calling for an **11% pay increase** for 967,000 Federal employees.

U.S. State Secretary John Foster Dulles announces that the existence of a Soviet ICBM does not initially affect the present "military balance" between the U.S.S.R. and the U.S.

Wednesday 28: From The Hit Parade: Debbie Reynolds' hit song "Tammy" is the #1 pop single. Reynolds sang the title tune in the film "Tammy and the Bachelor" starring Leslie Nielsen, released earlier this year.

Inventor **Edgar Longaker**, 75, dies in Norristown, Pennsylvania. Longaker is best known for his invention of the "auto ignition battery".

Thursday 29: Warner Brothers premieres its new musical comedy film **"The Pajama Game"** starring Doris Day, Eddy Foy Jr., John Raitt, Carol Haney. The film is based on Richard Bissell's best-selling book and successful Broadway play.

Friday 30: The **85th United States Congress** adjourns its first session, recessing until January 7th, 1958. During this historic 8-month session Congress has passed some 250 public laws including the first major civil rights action to protect voting rights, which now moves to White House for approval.

Saturday 31: Close to 60% of all television networks have converted their stations to receive **color transmissions**. NBC-TV has introduced its new color logo, a beautiful peacock. NBC chose the "peacock" over its second choice a "flag" and a third choice a "butterfly" to be the Network logo.

Debbie Reynolds has the #1 hit song "Tammy". (See August 28th)

Motorola's new Calypso "Portable" Player in two-tone Jamaican sand and ivory sells for $79.95.

The "Edsel" is introduced. (See August 26th)

EDSEL

SEPTEMBER *1957*

Black students enter Central High School in Little Rock, Arkansas.

SUNDAY	MONDAY	TUESDAY	WEDNESDAY	THURSDAY	FRIDAY	SATURDAY

1 With tensions running high over the prospect of a World nuclear castastrophe, over 200,000 pack N.Y. City's Broadway District for a farewell rally by Reverend Billy Graham as the fiery Evangelist concludes an historic 4-day rally in the nation's biggest city.

2 A total of 636 Americans lost their lives over the Labor Day weekend, including 445 traffic accident deaths and 95 drownings.

Disaster strikes Jamaica as a excursion train plunges into a ravine killing over 200 people and injuring hundreds of others.

3 President Eisenhower plans no early intervention in the Little Rock School integration situation. Eisenhower, citing people's emotions about segregationism, reiterates that "you cannot change people's hearts merely by making laws".

4 Arkansas Governor Orval Faubus orders the National Guard to prevent 9 black students from entering the all-white Central High School in Little Rock. A large crowd jeers at the students but no violence occurs.

5 Cuban President Fulgencio Batista's Army soundly defeats a major uprising led by revolutionist Fidel Castro in a battle less than 150 miles from Havana. It is the second time in the last 9 months an overthrow attempt by Castro has been squashed.

6 Officials for the U.S. Lawn Tennis Association disapprove a proposal that would have allowed Tennis Tournaments where professionals could compete against the best amateurs.

7 University of Colorado's Marilyn Van Derbur, 20, wins the 31st "Miss America" Beauty Pageant in Atlantic City. "Miss Georgia" is the first runner-up. Marilyn Van Derbur is the second "Miss America" to come from Colorado.

8 Althea Gibson, 30, defeats Louise Brough 6-3, 6-2, to become the first black in 71 Open Championships ever to win the United States Open Women's Singles Tennis Championship. Australia's Malcolm Anderson, 22, defeats fellow-Australian Ashley Cooper, 20, to take the Men's Singles title.

9 The average annual wage per working person in the United States for this year is $4,546.

The #1 song on the Country and Western music chart is "Whole Lot Of Shakin' Going On" by Jerry Lee Lewis.

10 Boris Pasternak's book "Dr. Zhivago" is published in Italy following unsuccessful attempts to secure publication in the U.S.S.R. The future best-selling book will eventually be developed into an Academy-Award-winning film starring Omar Shariff.

11 From The Hit Parade:
The #1 U.S. pop single for just this week is "Diana" by Paul Anka.

TV Programs Tonight On CBS:
7:30 I Love Lucy
8:00 The Big Record
9:00 The Millionaire
9:30 I've Got A Secret
10:00 The U.S. Steel Hour

12 CBS-TV premieres a second format of the original "Lassie" show, renamed "Timmy and Lassie". "Timmy Martin" is played by Jon Provost who lives with adoptive parents "Ruth & Paul Martin". Ruth is played first by Cloris Leachman and later by June Lockhart. "Paul Martin" is played by Jon Shepodd.

13 John Hopkins Medical Researcher, Dr. Winston Price, 33, is reported to have developed a vaccine proven to be successful in preventing the common cold that is caused by a JH virus. According to medical authorities JH viruses are responsible for close to 30% of all common colds.

14 The 57th U.S. National Amateur Golf Championship is won by Hillman Robbins Jr. over Dr. Frank M. Taylor at the Country Club near Brookline, Massachusetts.

CBS-TV premieres a new western series "Have Gun, Will Travel" starring Richard Boone as "Paladin", a gunman "For Hire".

15 CBS-TV premieres a new comedy "Bachelor Party" about a bachelor, played by John Forsythe, an attorney who has custody of his orphaned 13-year-old niece, and his trials of raising her with the help of his Chinese houseboy "Peter Tong".

16 Utica, Kansas: School Superintendent Bill Sallee, 55, dies in a bizarre accident when he accidentally hangs himself while imitating the part of a man being hanged during a high school freshmen initiation.

17 The American Motors Company announces that it has decided to discontinue both the "Nash" and "Hudson" automobiles. The company plans to place more focus on building lower-priced "Ramblers".

CBS-TV premieres "The Eve Arden Show". Following the cancellation of "Our Miss Brooks", Eve Arden returns in a new situation comedy.

18 NBC-TV premieres a new western series about a wagon train journey to California in 1880. "Wagon Train" stars Ward Bond as "Seth Adams" the Wagon Master, Robert Horton as "Flint McCullough" the first scout, with Terry Wilson and Robert Fullers as other trail scouts.

19 The #1 song on the Country and Western music chart is shared by Bobby Helm's hit "Fraulein" and Ray Price's hit "My Shoes Keep Walking Back To You".

TV Programs Tonight On ABC:
8:30 The Real McCoys
9:00 The Pat Boone Show
9:30 O.S.S.

20 Los Angeles: Undisputed World Light-Heavyweight Champion, Archie Moore, defends his title for the 6th time as he knocks out fellow-American Tony Anthony, 22.

NBC-TV premieres a new mystery series, "The Thin Man", starring Peter Lawford.

21 CBS-TV premieres a new drama, "Perry Mason", based on the courtroom trials of mastermind lawyer "Perry Mason", played by Raymond Burr. His beautiful secretary "Della Street" (Barbara Hale) and private detective "Paul Drake" (William Hopper) assist him to outwit prosecutor "Hamilton Burger" (William Talman).

22 ABC-TV premieres a new western series, "Maverick". The 1880's frontier story features exploits of two gentlemen gamblers. James Garner and Jack Kelly play "Bret" and "Bart Maverick". The cast includes Roger Moore as a British cousin and Efrem Zimbalist Jr. as a con artist friend.

23 9 black children enter Little Rock's Central High School to begin desegregated classes. Three days ago, a court ordered Arkansas Gov. Orval Faubus to remove the National Guard Troops that barred blacks from the school. 3 hours later the children were sent home when a mob of 1,000 gathered.

24 President Eisenhower issues an executive order directing Defense Secretary Charles Wilson to federalize the Arkansas National Guard. The order authorizes him to use whatever military force is necessary to prevent obstruction of a court order which allows 9 black children into the Central High School.

25 Under the protection of the 101st Division of the National Guard, 9 black children re-enter Central High School in Little Rock, Arkansas. An angry mob cheers while many students leave the school in protest of their admission. Several women and young girls *scream in hysteria* over their admission.

26 20th Century-Fox releases the film "Three Faces of Eve" starring Joanne Woodward as a young woman with three personalities, with co-stars Lee J. Cobb and David Wayne. Woodward will win a "Best Actress Oscar" for her performance.

27 From The Hit Parade:
The #1 U.S. pop single is The Crickets' song "That'll Be The Day". The Crickets, led by Buddy Holly, recorded the song last February while in New Mexico.

28 The Milwaukee Braves of the National Baseball League end their first pennant-winning season with a 95-59 record, 8 games ahead of the 2nd place St. Louis Cardinals. Managed by Fred Haney, the Braves are led by Henry "Hank" Aaron, 23, who hit 44 homers, and Eddie Mathews who hit 33.

29 MLB Season Leaders:
Batting: NL - Stan Musial (St.L.) .351 (7th time)
AL - Ted Williams (Bost) .388 (5th time)
HR's: NL - Hank Aaron (Milw) 44
AL - Roy Sievers (Wash) 42
RBI's: NL - Hank Aaron 132
AL - Roy Sievers 114

30 The powerful New York Yankees, managed by Casey Stengel, conclude the American League regular season, winning their 8th pennant in 9 years, finishing with a 98-56 record. The well-balanced Yankees are led by 25-year-old sensation Mickey Mantle who hit .365 while pounding out 34 home runs.

James Garner and Jack Kelly star as "Bret and Bart Maverick" in the new television series "Maverick". (See September 22nd)

Richard Boone stars as "Paladin" in the new TV western series "Have Gun, Will Travel". (See September 14th)

Raymond Burr and Barbara Hale star in the new TV drama series "Perry Mason". (See September 21st)

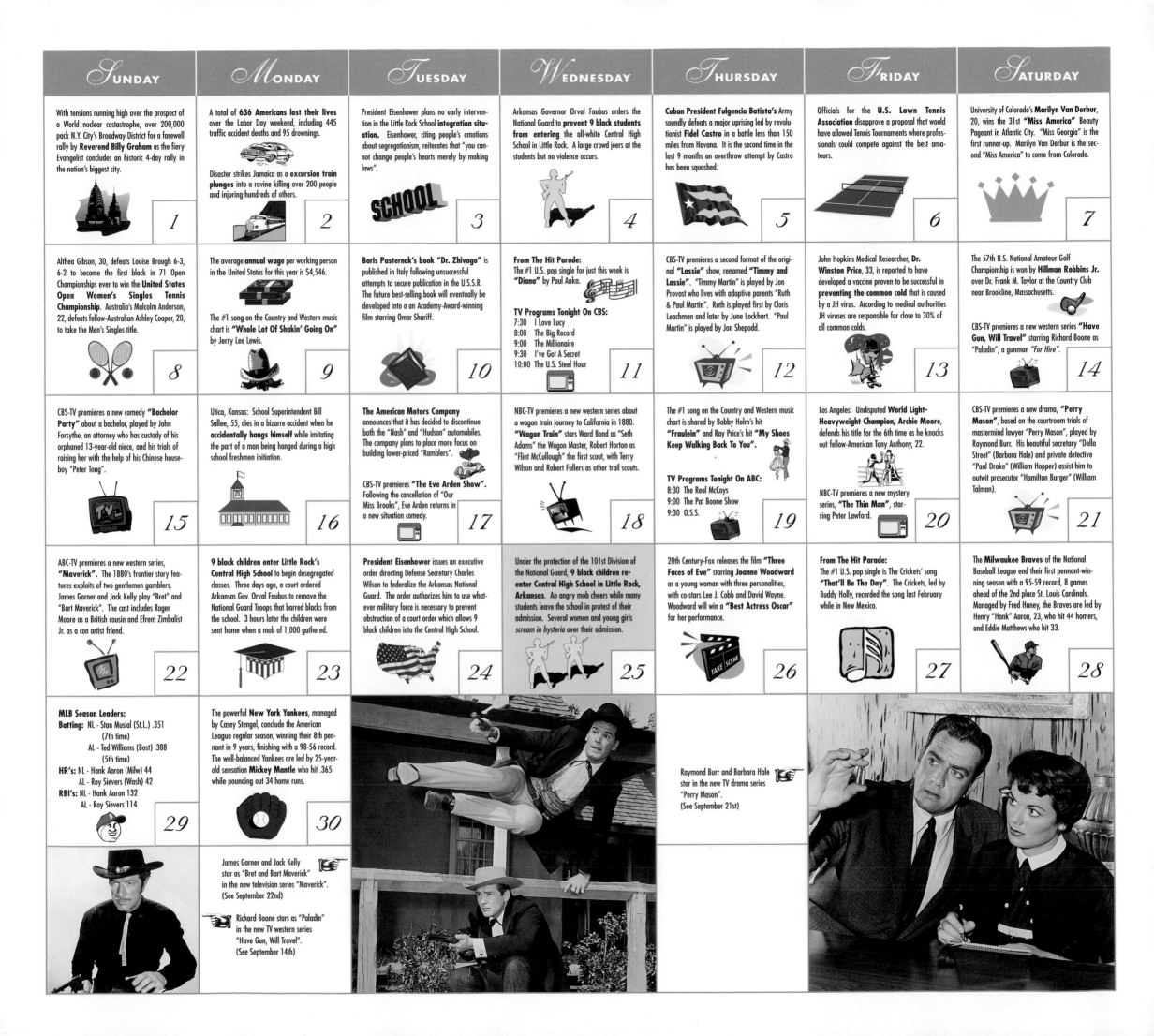

Milwaukee Braves - 1957 World Series Champions

Sunday

NY Yankee rookie Tony Kubek hits two home runs in game 3 of the World Series.
(See October 5th)

Monday

1

A new play, **"Look Back In Anger"**, written by John Osborne, opens at The Lyceum Theater in N.Y.C. with Kenneth Haigh, Alan Bates, Mary Ure, Vivienne Drummond and Jack Livesy. The play will run for 407 performances.

TV Programs Tonight On ABC:
7:30 Cheyenne
8:30 Wyatt Earp
9:00 Broken Arrow
9:30 Telephone Time

Tuesday

2

The **New York Yankees** edge the **Milwaukee Braves** 3-1 to win game one of the 54th Annual World Series Baseball Championships. Left-hander Whitey Ford, 28, pitches a complete game for the victory.

Wednesday

3

The visiting **Milwaukee Braves** edge the **Yankees** 4-2 to even their World Series of Baseball at one game apiece.

ABC-TV features **"The Woody Woodpecker Show"**. The Walter Lantz creation includes "Woody" and his cast of characters "Andy Panda", "Space Mouse" and "Gabby Gator". The voice of Woody Woodpecker is none other than creator Lantz's wife Gracie.

Thursday

4

The Soviet Union space program successfully launches the **first artificial earth satellite "Sputnik"**. Tass reports that the 184-lb satellite reaches an altitude of 560 miles, attaining a velocity of 18,000 mph. The satellite, in an elliptical trajectory, takes 96 minutes to complete a revolution of the globe.

Jimmy Hoffa, 44, is elected President of the International Brotherhood of Teamsters.

Friday

5

The visiting **NY Yankees** slam the Milwaukee Braves 12-3 in the World Series led by two home runs by rookie Tony Kubek's . Mickey Mantle also hits one out for the Yankees who drew 13 walks. Pitcher Bob Turley records the win.

Great Britain, led by Dai Rees, wins the **12th Ryder Cup Golf Challenge** at the Lindrick, England, course.

Sunday

6

The home-field Braves edge NY 7-5 to even the World Series at 2 games apiece. The dramatic contest is tied 4-4 in the 10th inning when the Yankees score the apparent winner in the top of the inning before the Braves rebound with 3 runs, the winning two on a 2-run home-run by Ed Mathews.

Monday

7

The Milwaukee Braves edge the Yankees 1-0 to take a 3-2 lead in the World Series as right-hander Lew Burdette tosses a 7-hit shutout.

TV Programs Tonight On CBS:
7:30 Robin Hood
8:00 Burns and Allen
8:30 Talent Scouts
9:00 Danny Thomas
9:30 December Bride

Tuesday

8

Brooklyn Dodger stockholders vote to move their team to Los Angeles for the 1958 season.

TV Programs Tonight On CBS:
7:30 Name That Tune
8:00 You'll Never Get Rich
8:30 The Eve Arden Show
9:00 To Tell The Truth
9:30 Red Skelton
10:00 The $64,000 Question
10:30 Assignment Foreign Legion

Wednesday

9

The home-field Yankees edge the Braves 3-2 on a 7th-inning home run by Hank Bauer. Yogi Berra scored the other runs earlier on a home run, with Joe Torre and Hank Aaron hitting homers for Milwaukee. Bob Turley tosses a 4-hit complete-game victory.

From the Hit Parade:
The # 1 song in the U.S. is "Honeycomb" by Jimmie Rodgers.

Thursday

10

The **Milwaukee Braves defeat the home-field Yankees 5-0 to win their first World Series**. Pitcher Selva Lewis "Lew" Burdette goes the distance, his 2nd consecutive shutout, to capture the "MVP" Honor, becoming the first since Harry Brecheen in 1946 in St. Louis to win 3 games in the same World Series.

Friday

11

CBS-TV has introduced its new sitcom **"Leave It To Beaver"**. The "Cleaver Family" includes "Theodore Beaver" (Jerry Mathers), his brother "Wally" (Tony Dow), mother "June" (Barbara Billingsley), and his father "Ward" (Hugh Beaumont). The soon-to-be "hit show" made its debut on October 4th.

TV Programs Tonight On ABC:
7:30 Cheyenne
8:30 Wyatt Earp

Saturday

12

Following a Sydney, Australia, rock concert, **Little Richard** announces his decision to give up "rock-and-roll" singing. He leaves for the United States to be baptized into the Seventh Day Adventist Faith.

TV Programs Tonight On ABC:
7:30 Keep It In The Family
8:00 Ozark Jubilee
9:00 The Lawrence Welk Show
10:00 Mike Wallace Interview

Sunday

13

RCA Victor has already received 500,000 advance orders for Elvis Presley's Christmas Album, of which only one half has been pressed. Presley's rock-and-roll image is considered by many groups to be a negative image for Christmas music.

Monday

14

The prestigious **Alfred B. Nobel Peace Prize** is awarded to future Canadian Prime Minister Lester B. Pearson.

President Dwight D. Eisenhower celebrates his **67th birthday** at the White House.

Tuesday

15

Arkansas **Governor Faubus** claims the withdrawal of 500 Federal troops from Little Rock will not bring a peaceful solution any closer.

Jimmy Hoffa pleads innocent in a Federal District Court in N.Y. City to charges that he had lied to a Federal Grand Jury investigating illegal wiretapping charges. Hoffa remains free under a $2,500 bond.

Wednesday

16

England's Queen Elizabeth and **Prince Philip** arrive in the U.S. to begin a six-day tour after visiting Canada. They visit the city of Jamestown which is regarded as the first permanent English new-world settlement which is enjoying its 350th anniversary celebrations.

Thursday

17

From The Hit Parade:
Keen Records releases a new record **"You Send Me"** backed by **"Summertime"** by Sam Cooke, the former gospel singer. The future best-seller and #1 hit will rack up over 2.6 million sales to Cooke's all-time best-selling record.

Friday

18

ABC-TV premieres the new western series **"Colt .45"** starring Wayde Preston as Government Agent "Christopher Colt" the son of the inventor of the colt .45 revolver.

From The Hit Parade:
The #1 pop song in the U.S. is "Wake Up, Little Susie" by the Everly Brothers.

Saturday

19

The National Hockey League's **Maurice "Rocket" Richard**, star of the Montreal Canadiens, becomes the first player to reach the 500-goal mark in a career as he scores against Glenn Hall at 15:52 of the first period in a game against the Chicago Black Hawks.

Sunday

20

"The 20th Century" documentary TV show narrated by Walter Cronkite premieres on the CBS Television Network. It will become a popular weekly program as Americans are walked through key historical 20th century events with film documentation.

Monday

21

The **United States Supreme Court refuses to reverse** an order issued by a Federal Judge in Virginia against delaying racial integration of public schools due to provisions of their Public Placement Act.

Tuesday

22

Two plastic bombs planted in front of a U.S. officer's quarters and under a bus carrying American enlisted men **explode in Saigon** injuring 13 U.S. soldiers along with 15 Vietnamese children.

Wednesday

23

The New York Stock Exchange enjoys its best day since November 14th, 1929. President Eisenhower points out that the economy overall is not moving into a depression but is, in fact, stabilizing after a lengthy surge.

Thursday

24

Entertainer **Bing Crosby**, 53, marries actress **Kathryn Grant**, 23, in Las Vegas, Nevada. It is the popular entertainer's 2nd marriage.

The #1 song on the Country and Western music chart is **"Wake Up, Little Susie"** by the Everly Brothers.

Friday

25

Albert Anastasia, 55, a New York gangster, is murdered by two hooded gunmen while sitting in a barber's chair at New York's Park Sheraton Hotel. Anastasia is believed to have killed 31 people for "Murder Inc.".

Saturday

26

The **U.S. Women's Basketball** team wins the World Championship final 51-48 over Russia in Rio de Janeiro.

TV Programs Tonight On CBS:
7:30 Perry Mason
8:30 Dick and the Duchess
9:00 Oh! Susanna
9:30 Have Gun, Will Travel
10:00 Gunsmoke

Sunday

27

The **5th Annual World Cup of Golf (Canada Cup)** held this year at the Kasumigaseki Country Club in Tokyo, Japan, is won for the first time by the golfers from Japan whose combined score of 557 edges the two-time defending champion United States by 9 strokes.

Monday

28

Boeing's first product Model 707 jet-powered airliner is completed in Seattle.

AFL-CIO leaders have voted to **suspend the International Brotherhood of Teamsters** unless the 1.5-million-member-union cleans up its act. Leaders will expel the Teamsters led by Jimmy Hoffa if changes are not immediately made. The Teamsters are accused of widespread corruption and abuses.

Tuesday

29

Pioneer movie producer **Louis B. Mayer**, 72, dies in Hollywood. Mayer, the MGM Vice-President until six years ago, is best known for his epic movies "Ben-Hur", "Dinner at Eight" and "Grand Hotel".

Wednesday

30

From the Hit Parade:
"Jailhouse Rock"/"Treat Me Nice" by Elvis Presley is the #1 pop single. The top album for the 4th week is the **"Around The World In Eighty Days"** film sound track.

Thursday

31

The prestigious **"Cy Young" Memorial Award** presented annually to Major League Baseball's **best pitcher**, as selected by the Baseball Writers of America, goes to National League Milwaukee Braves star **Warren Spahn**. The 36-year-old left-hander won 21 games while losing just 11 with an ERA of 2.69.

(Far Left)
New Sears portable radio with Magic-Disk Antenna sells for $29.95.

Children's phonograph

Tony Dow and Jerry Mathers star in the new TV sitcom "Leave It To Beaver". (See October 11th)

$29⁹⁵

Magic-Disk

AROUND THE WORLD IN 80 DAYS
Michael Todd's
MCA RECORDS

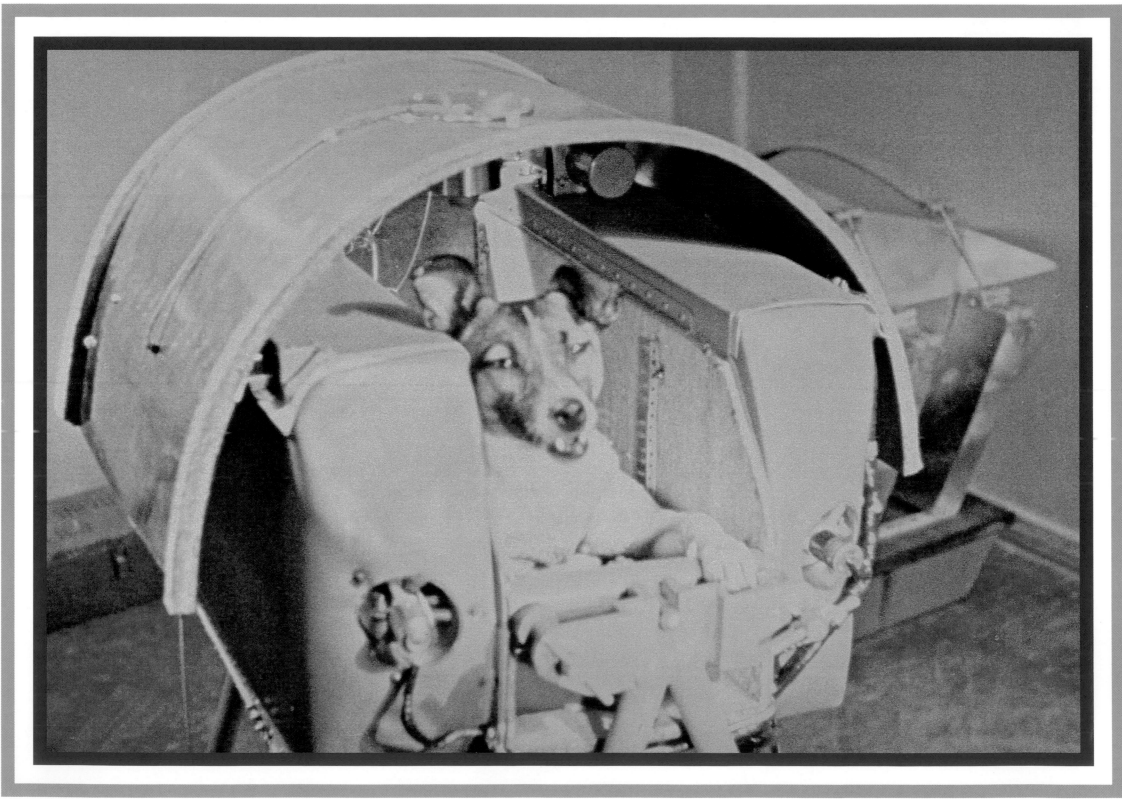

The earth's first space traveler "Laika" the Dog.

Sunday	Monday	Tuesday	Wednesday	Thursday	Friday	Saturday

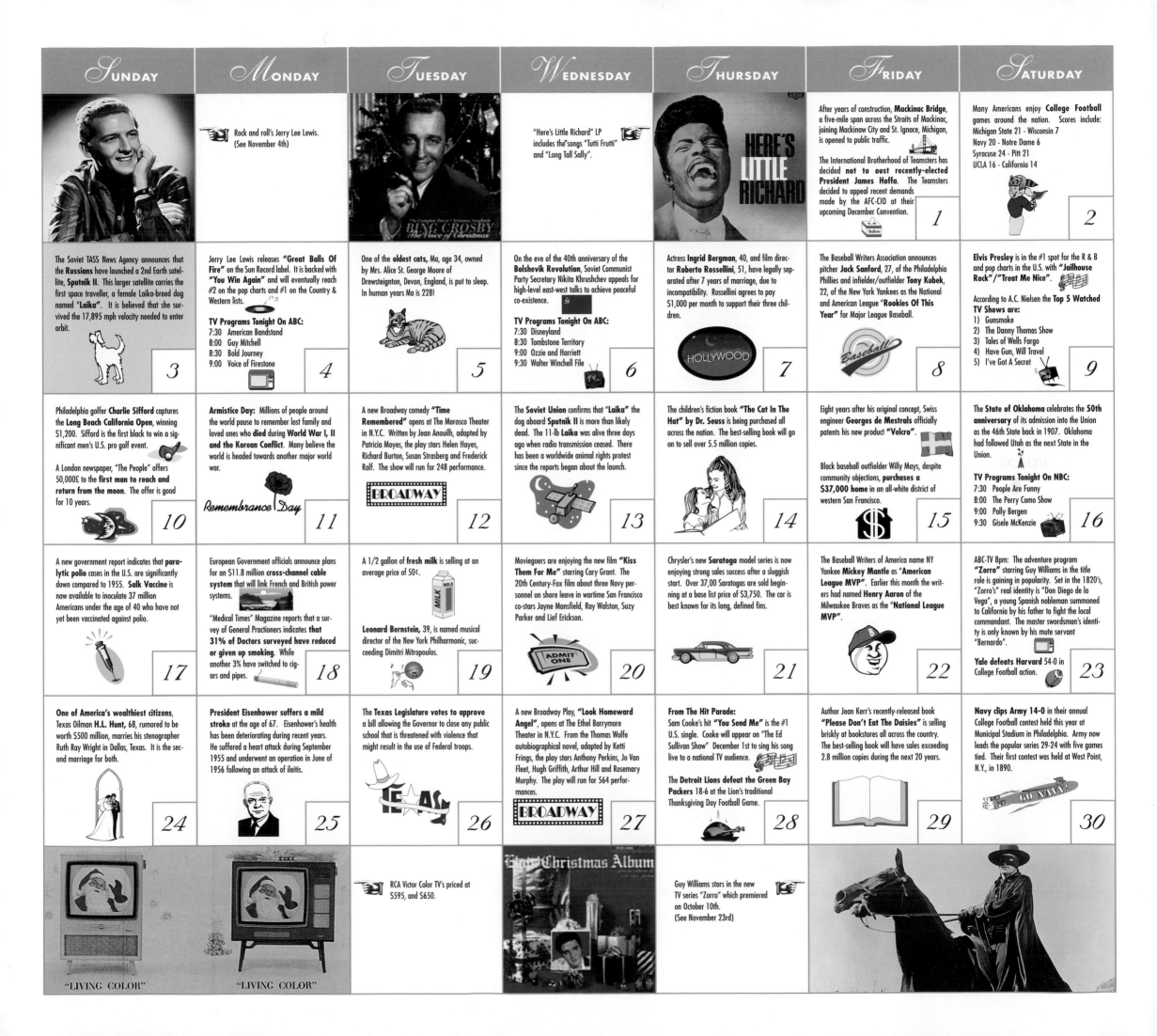

Monday: Rock and roll's Jerry Lee Lewis. (See November 4th)

Tuesday: "Here's Little Richard" LP includes the songs "Tutti Frutti" and "Long Tall Sally".

Friday 1: After years of construction, **Mackinac Bridge**, a five-mile span across the Straits of Mackinac, joining Mackinaw City and St. Ignace, Michigan, is opened to public traffic.

The International Brotherhood of Teamsters has decided **not to oust recently-elected President James Hoffa**. The Teamsters decided to appeal recent demands made by the AFC-CIO at their upcoming December Convention.

Saturday 2: Many Americans enjoy **College Football** games around the nation. Scores include:
Michigan State 21 - Wisconsin 7
Navy 20 - Notre Dame 6
Syracuse 24 - Pitt 21
UCLA 16 - California 14

3: The Soviet TASS News Agency announces that the **Russians** have launched a 2nd Earth satellite, **Sputnik II**. This larger satellite carries the first space traveller, a female Laika-breed dog named "**Laika**". It is believed that she survived the 17,895 mph velocity needed to enter orbit.

4: Jerry Lee Lewis releases "**Great Balls Of Fire**" on the Sun Record label. It is backed with "**You Win Again**" and will eventually reach #2 on the pop charts and #1 on the Country & Western lists.

TV Programs Tonight On ABC:
7:30 American Bandstand
8:00 Guy Mitchell
8:30 Bold Journey
9:00 Voice of Firestone

5: One of the **oldest cats**, Ma, age 34, owned by Mrs. Alice St. George Moore of Drewsteignton, Devon, England, is put to sleep. In human years Ma is 228!

6: On the eve of the 40th anniversary of the **Bolshevik Revolution**, Soviet Communist Party Secretary Nikita Khrushchev appeals for high-level east-west talks to achieve peaceful co-existence.

TV Programs Tonight On ABC:
7:30 Disneyland
8:30 Tombstone Territory
9:00 Ozzie and Harriett
9:30 Walter Winchell File

7: Actress **Ingrid Bergman**, 40, and film director **Roberto Rossellini**, 51, have legally separated after 7 years of marriage, due to incompatibility. Rossellini agrees to pay $1,000 per month to support their three children.

8: The Baseball Writers Association announces pitcher **Jack Sanford**, 27, of the Philadelphia Phillies and infielder/outfielder **Tony Kubek**, 22, of the New York Yankees as the National and American League "**Rookies Of This Year**" for Major League Baseball.

9: **Elvis Presley** is in the #1 spot for the R & B and pop charts in the U.S. with "**Jailhouse Rock**"/"**Treat Me Nice**".

According to A.C. Nielsen the **Top 5 Watched TV Shows** are:
1) Gunsmoke
2) The Danny Thomas Show
3) Tales of Wells Fargo
4) Have Gun, Will Travel
5) I've Got A Secret

10: Philadelphia golfer **Charlie Sifford** captures the **Long Beach California Open**, winning $1,200. Sifford is the first black to win a significant men's U.S. pro golf event.

A London newspaper, "The People" offers 50,000£ to the **first man to reach and return from the moon**. The offer is good for 10 years.

11: **Armistice Day:** Millions of people around the world pause to remember lost family and loved ones who **died during World War I, II and the Korean Conflict.** Many believe the world is headed towards another major world war.

Remembrance Day

12: A new Broadway comedy "**Time Remembered**" opens at The Morosco Theater in N.Y.C. Written by Jean Anouilh, adapted by Patricia Moyes, the play stars Helen Hayes, Richard Burton, Susan Strasberg and Frederick Rolf. The show will run for 248 performances.

BROADWAY

13: The **Soviet Union** confirms that "**Laika**" the dog aboard Sputnik II is more than likely dead. The 11-lb Laika was alive three days ago when radio transmission ceased. There has been a worldwide animal rights protest since the reports began about the launch.

14: The children's fiction book "**The Cat In The Hat**" by Dr. Seuss is being purchased all across the nation. The best-selling book will go on to sell over 5.5 million copies.

15: Eight years after his original concept, Swiss engineer **Georges de Mestrals** officially patents his new product "**Velcro**".

Black baseball outfielder **Willy Mays**, despite community objections, **purchases a $37,000 home** in an all-white district of western San Francisco.

16: The **State of Oklahoma** celebrates the **50th anniversary** of its admission into the Union as the 46th State back in 1907. Oklahoma had followed Utah as the next State in the Union.

TV Programs Tonight On NBC:
7:30 People Are Funny
8:00 The Perry Como Show
9:00 Polly Bergen
9:30 Gisele McKenzie

17: A new government report indicates that **paralytic polio** cases in the U.S. are significantly down compared to 1955. **Salk Vaccine** is now available to inoculate 37 million Americans under the age of 40 who have not yet been vaccinated against polio.

18: European Government officials announce plans for an $11.8 million **cross-channel cable system** that will link French and British power systems.

"Medical Times" Magazine reports that a survey of General Practioners indicates **that 31% of Doctors surveyed have reduced or given up smoking.** While another 3% have switched to cigars and pipes.

19: A 1/2 gallon of **fresh milk** is selling at an average price of 50¢.

MILK

Leonard Bernstein, 39, is named musical director of the New York Philharmonic, succeeding Dimitri Mitropoulos.

20: Moviegoers are enjoying the new film "**Kiss Them For Me**" starring Cary Grant. The 20th Century-Fox film about three Navy personnel on shore leave in wartime San Francisco co-stars Jayne Mansfield, Ray Walston, Suzy Parker and Lief Erickson.

ADMIT ONE

21: Chrysler's new **Saratoga** model series is now enjoying strong sales success after a sluggish start. Over 37,00 Saratogas are sold beginning at a base list price of $3,750. The car is best known for its long, defined fins.

22: The Baseball Writers of America name NY Yankee **Mickey Mantle** as "**American League MVP**". Earlier this month the writers had named **Henry Aaron** of the Milwaukee Braves as the "**National League MVP**".

23: ABC-TV 8pm: The adventure program "**Zorro**" starring Guy Williams in the title role is gaining in popularity. Set in the 1820's, "Zorro's" real identity is "Don Diego de la Vega", a young Spanish nobleman summoned to California by his father to fight the local commandant. The master swordsman's identity is only known by his mute servant "Bernardo".

Yale defeats Harvard 54-0 in College Football action.

24: One of America's wealthiest citizens, Texas Oilman **H.L. Hunt**, 68, rumored to be worth $500 million, marries his stenographer Ruth Ray Wright in Dallas, Texas. It is the second marriage for both.

25: President Eisenhower suffers a mild **stroke** at the age of 67. Eisenhower's health has been deteriorating during recent years. He suffered a heart attack during September 1955 and underwent an operation in June of 1956 following an attack of ileitis.

26: The Texas Legislature votes to approve a bill allowing the Governor to close any public school that is threatened with violence that might result in the use of Federal troops.

TEXAS

27: A new Broadway Play, "**Look Homeward Angel**", opens at The Ethel Barrymore Theater in N.Y.C. From the Thomas Wolfe autobiographical novel, adapted by Ketti Frings, the play stars Anthony Perkins, Jo Van Fleet, Hugh Griffith, Arthur Hill and Rosemary Murphy. The play will run for 564 performances.

BROADWAY

28: **From The Hit Parade:** Sam Cooke's hit "**You Send Me**" is the #1 U.S. single. Cooke will appear on "The Ed Sullivan Show" December 1st to sing his song live to a national TV audience.

The **Detroit Lions defeat the Green Bay Packers** 18-6 at the Lion's traditional Thanksgiving Day Football Game.

29: Author Jean Kerr's recently-released book "**Please Don't Eat the Daisies**" is selling briskly at bookstores all across the country. The best-selling book will have sales exceeding 2.8 million copies during the next 20 years.

30: **Navy** clips **Army** 14-0 in their annual College Football contest held this year at Municipal Stadium in Philadelphia. Army now leads the popular series 29-24 with five games tied. Their first contest was held at West Point, N.Y., in 1890.

GO NAVY!

"LIVING COLOR"

"LIVING COLOR"

RCA Victor Color TV's priced at $595, and $650.

Elvis' Christmas Album

Guy Williams stars in the new TV series "Zorro" which premiered on October 10th. (See November 23rd)

Marlon Brando, Miiko Taka, Miyoshi Umeki and Red Buttons from the new film "Sayonara".

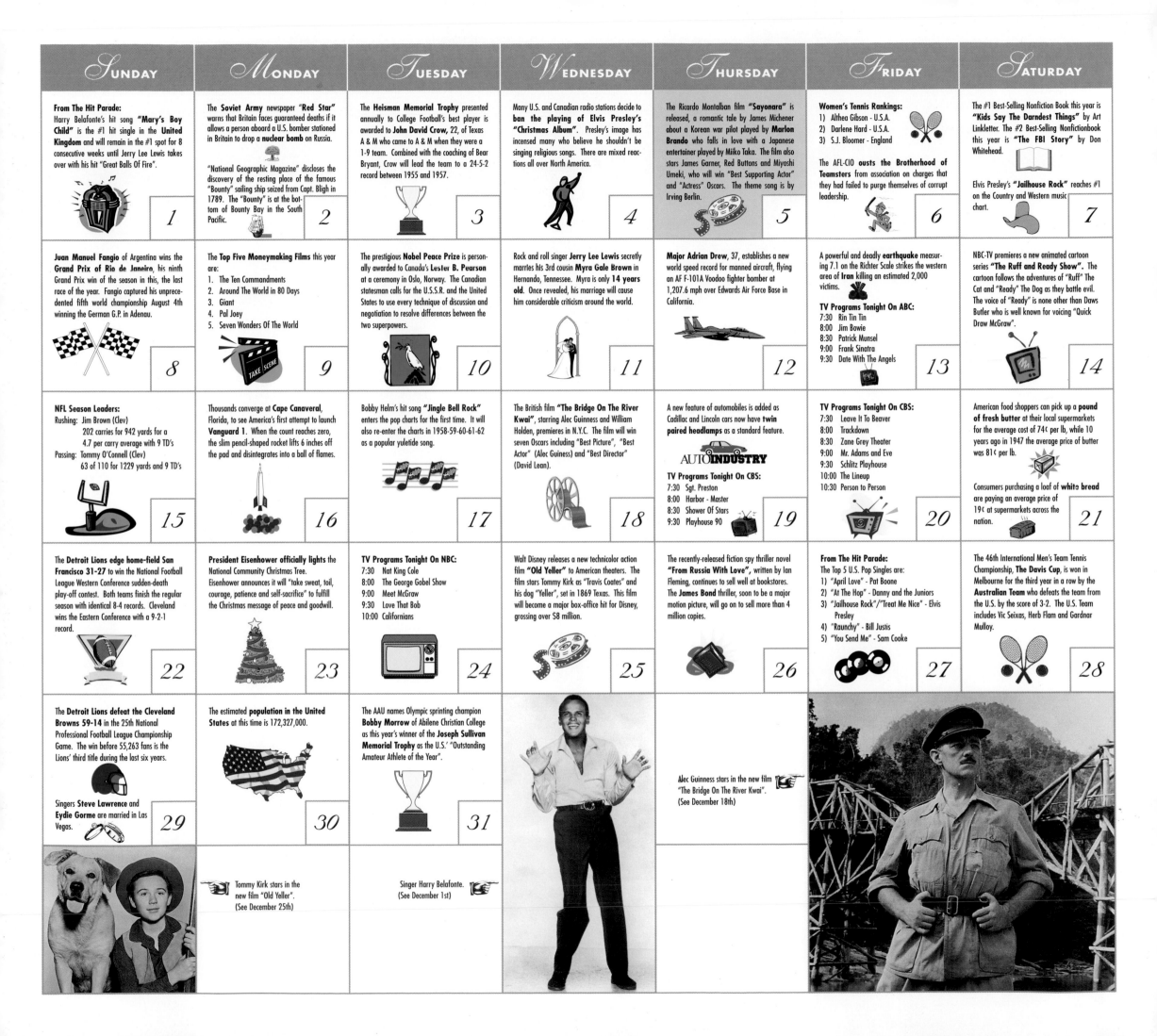

Sunday	Monday	Tuesday	Wednesday	Thursday	Friday	Saturday

From The Hit Parade:
Harry Belafonte's hit song **"Mary's Boy Child"** is the #1 hit single in the **United Kingdom** and will remain in the #1 spot for 8 consecutive weeks until Jerry Lee Lewis takes over with his hit "Great Balls Of Fire". **1**

The **Soviet Army** newspaper "Red Star" warns that Britain faces guaranteed deaths if it allows a person aboard a U.S. bomber stationed in Britain to drop a **nuclear bomb** on Russia.

"National Geographic Magazine" discloses the discovery of the resting place of the famous "Bounty" sailing ship seized from Capt. Bligh in 1789. The "Bounty" is at the bottom of Bounty Bay in the South Pacific. **2**

The **Heisman Memorial Trophy** presented annually to College Football's best player is awarded to **John David Crow**, 22, of Texas A & M who came to A & M when they were a 1-9 team. Combined with the coaching of Bear Bryant, Crow will lead the team to a 24-5-2 record between 1955 and 1957. **3**

Many U.S. and Canadian radio stations decide to **ban the playing of Elvis Presley's "Christmas Album"**. Presley's image has incensed many who believe he shouldn't be singing religious songs. There are mixed reactions all over North America. **4**

The Ricardo Montalban film **"Sayonara"** is released, a romantic tale by James Michener about a Korean war pilot played by **Marlon Brando** who falls in love with a Japanese entertainer played by Miiko Taka. The film also stars James Garner, Red Buttons and Miyoshi Umeki, who will win "Best Supporting Actor" and "Actress" Oscars. The theme song is by Irving Berlin. **5**

Women's Tennis Rankings:
1) Althea Gibson - U.S.A.
2) Darlene Hard - U.S.A.
3) S.J. Bloomer - England

The **AFL-CIO ousts the Brotherhood of Teamsters** from association on charges that they had failed to purge themselves of corrupt leadership. **6**

The **#1 Best-Selling Nonfiction Book** this year is **"Kids Say The Darndest Things"** by Art Linkletter. The **#2 Best-Selling Nonfiction** book this year is **"The FBI Story"** by Don Whitehead.

Elvis Presley's **"Jailhouse Rock"** reaches #1 on the Country and Western music chart. **7**

Juan Manuel Fangio of Argentina wins the **Grand Prix of Rio de Janeiro**, his ninth Grand Prix win of the season in this, the last race of the year. Fangio captured his unprecedented fifth world championship August 4th winning the German G.P. in Adenau. **8**

The **Top Five Moneymaking Films** this year are:
1. The Ten Commandments
2. Around The World in 80 Days
3. Giant
4. Pal Joey
5. Seven Wonders Of The World **9**

The prestigious **Nobel Peace Prize** is personally awarded to Canada's **Lester B. Pearson** at a ceremony in Oslo, Norway. The Canadian statesman calls for the U.S.S.R. and the United States to use every technique of discussion and negotiation to resolve differences between the two superpowers. **10**

Rock and roll singer **Jerry Lee Lewis** secretly marries his 3rd cousin **Myra Gale Brown** in Hernando, Tennessee. Myra is only **14 years old**. Once revealed, his marriage will cause him considerable criticism around the world. **11**

Major Adrian Drew, 37, establishes a new world speed record for manned aircraft, flying an AF F-101A Voodoo fighter bomber at 1,207.6 mph over Edwards Air Force Base in California. **12**

A powerful and deadly **earthquake** measuring 7.1 on the Richter Scale strikes the western area of **Iran** killing an estimated 2,000 victims.

TV Programs Tonight On ABC:
7:30 Rin Tin Tin
8:00 Jim Bowie
8:30 Patrick Munsel
9:00 Frank Sinatra
9:30 Date With The Angels **13**

NBC-TV premieres a new animated cartoon series **"The Ruff and Ready Show"**. The cartoon follows the adventures of "Ruff" The Cat and "Ready" The Dog as they battle evil. The voice of "Ready" is none other than Daws Butler who is well known for voicing "Quick Draw McGraw". **14**

NFL Season Leaders:
Rushing: Jim Brown (Clev) 202 carries for 942 yards for a 4.7 per carry average with 9 TD's
Passing: Tommy O'Connell (Clev) 63 of 110 for 1229 yards and 9 TD's **15**

Thousands converge at **Cape Canaveral**, Florida, to see America's first attempt to launch **Vanguard 1**. When the count reaches zero, the slim pencil-shaped rocket lifts 6 inches off the pad and disintegrates into a ball of flames. **16**

Bobby Helm's hit song **"Jingle Bell Rock"** enters the pop charts for the first time. It will also re-enter the charts in 1958-59-60-61-62 as a popular yuletide song. **17**

The British film **"The Bridge On The River Kwai"**, starring Alec Guinness and William Holden, premieres in N.Y.C. The film will win seven Oscars including "Best Picture", "Best Actor" (Alec Guiness) and "Best Director" (David Lean). **18**

A new feature of automobiles is added as Cadillac and Lincoln cars now have **twin paired headlamps** as a standard feature.

AUTO INDUSTRY

TV Programs Tonight On CBS:
7:30 Sgt. Preston
8:00 Harbor - Master
8:30 Shower Of Stars
9:30 Playhouse 90 **19**

TV Programs Tonight On CBS:
7:30 Leave It To Beaver
8:00 Trackdown
8:30 Zane Grey Theater
9:00 Mr. Adams and Eve
9:30 Schlitz Playhouse
10:00 The Lineup
10:30 Person to Person **20**

American food shoppers can pick up a **pound of fresh butter** at their local supermarket for the average cost of 74¢ per lb, while 10 years ago in 1947 the average price of butter was 81¢ per lb.

Consumers purchasing a loaf of **white bread** are paying an average price of 19¢ at supermarkets across the nation. **21**

The Detroit Lions edge home-field San Francisco 31-27 to win the National Football League Western Conference sudden-death play-off contest. Both teams finish the regular season with identical 8-4 records. Cleveland wins the Eastern Conference with a 9-2-1 record. **22**

President Eisenhower officially lights the National Community Christmas Tree. Eisenhower announces it will "take sweat, toil, courage, patience and self-sacrifice" to fulfill the Christmas message of peace and goodwill. **23**

TV Programs Tonight On NBC:
7:30 Nat King Cole
8:00 The George Gobel Show
9:00 Meet McGraw
9:30 Love That Bob
10:00 Californians **24**

Walt Disney releases a new technicolor action film **"Old Yeller"** to American theaters. The film stars Tommy Kirk as "Travis Coates" and his dog "Yeller", set in 1869 Texas. This film will become a major box-office hit for Disney, grossing over $8 million. **25**

The recently-released fiction spy thriller novel **"From Russia With Love"**, written by Ian Fleming, continues to sell well at bookstores. The **James Bond** thriller, soon to be a major motion picture, will go on to sell more than 4 million copies. **26**

From The Hit Parade:
The Top 5 U.S. Pop Singles are:
1) "April Love" - Pat Boone
2) "At The Hop" - Danny and the Juniors
3) "Jailhouse Rock"/"Treat Me Nice" - Elvis Presley
4) "Raunchy" - Bill Justis
5) "You Send Me" - Sam Cooke **27**

The 46th International Men's Team Tennis Championship, **The Davis Cup**, is won in Melbourne for the third year in a row by the **Australian Team** who defeats the team from the U.S. by the score of 3-2. The U.S. Team includes Vic Seixas, Herb Flam and Gardnar Mulloy. **28**

The Detroit Lions defeat the Cleveland Browns **59-14** in the 25th National Professional Football League Championship Game. The win before 55,263 fans is the Lions' third title during the last six years.

Singers **Steve Lawrence** and **Eydie Gorme** are married in Las Vegas. **29**

The estimated **population in the United States** at this time is 172,327,000. **30**

The AAU names Olympic sprinting champion **Bobby Morrow** of Abilene Christian College as this year's winner of the **Joseph Sullivan Memorial Trophy** as the U.S.' "Outstanding Amateur Athlete of the Year". **31**

Tommy Kirk stars in the new film "Old Yeller". (See December 25th)

Singer Harry Belafonte. (See December 1st)

Alec Guinness stars in the new film "The Bridge On The River Kwai". (See December 18th)